Barbie™

FOREVER

Her Inspiration, History, and Legacy

FOREVER

Her Inspiration, History, and Legacy

ROBIN GERBER

EPIC INK

Brimming with creative inspiration, how-to projects, and useful information to enrich your everyday life, Quarto Knows is a favorite destination for those pursuing their interests and passions. Visit our site and dig deeper with our books into your area of interest: Quarto Creates, Quarto Cooks, Quarto Homes, Quarto Lives, Quarto Drives, Quarto Explores, Quarto Gifts, or Quarto Kids.

BARBIE and associated trademarks and trade dress are owned by and used under license from Mattel. ©2019 Mattel, Inc.

Published in 2019 by Epic Ink, an imprint of The Quarto Group
1120 NE 33rd Place, Suite 201, Bellevue, Washington 98004
www.QuartoKnows.com

19 20 21 22 23   5 4 3 2 1

ISBN: 978-0-7603-6577-9

Author: Robin Gerber
Editorial: Bonnie Honeycutt
Design: Megan Sugiyama
Production: Tom Miller

Printed, manufactured, and assembled in China 06/19.

305204

CONTENTS

FOREWORD

Barbie and I go way back. Growing up in Maplewood, New Jersey, I had tons of Barbie dolls that I played with. I even had the three-story Barbie Dream House and the Barbie Corvette.

One thing I loved about my Barbie dolls was that they were all shades of brown, which was my mom's way of ensuring that my sisters and I saw our own beauty represented in doll play. I would even find little scraps of fabric lying around the house from my mom's crafts, so that my dolls could wear a hijab like me.

When I played with Barbie, I remember imagining myself as an emergency room doctor, or a busy mom, or even a race car driver in my little pink Corvette. My sisters and I would act out different adventures, anywhere our big imaginations could take us. I held onto those endless dreams and the possibilities of what I could become.

I never imagined when I was playing with Barbie twenty years ago that this brand would be honoring someone like me—a fencer in hijab who embraced what made me different. I am honored and humbled, not only because I have a doll that looks like me, but for what Barbie means to me. It is a celebration of breaking boundaries and expanding possibilities of girls everywhere. I worked closely with the Barbie team to ensure my Barbie had strong legs and a hijab like mine, and the perfect winged eyeliner, of course. Barbie serves as a reminder to our girls that they too have the power to embrace what makes them different.

Barbie represents the fearlessness and boundless imagination we all hope to achieve in our lives. She continues to evolve, and to highlight the importance of pushing diversity and inclusivity to the forefront. It is my hope that Barbie continues to encourage boys and girls everywhere to embrace what makes them different and inspires the next generation to dream fearlessly!

May your faith be greater than your fears.

—Ibtihaj Muhammad
Olympic Medalist with the United States Fencing Team

OPPOSITE: Ibtihaj Muhammad, an American sabre fencer and member of the United States fencing team who earned a bronze medal at the 2016 Summer Olympics, poses with a Shero Barbie made in her likeness, celebrating and honoring her as a woman who has broken boundaries to inspire the next generation of girls.

INTRODUCTION

Although I wrote the biography of Ruth Handler, entitled *Barbie and Ruth*, I would not have called myself a Barbie expert when I received the request asking me to write this book. What interested me most about Barbie was her creator, an entrepreneurial genius and pioneering woman who founded the biggest toy company in the world: Mattel. Ruth's high concept—that little girls just want to play at being big girls—fascinated me, and this book gave me the chance to answer some of the big questions that had trailed me since writing Ruth's biography: How had Barbie lasted this long? And how long could she go on?

My journey led me to Mattel headquarters in El Segundo, California, and the Barbie brand staff, who work out of what seems like an old airplane hangar. In the enormous space, now decorated with the wild and rich imagination of an army of creators, I learned about who Barbie is today.

As the designers, artists, marketers, and managers explained Barbie at sixty, I kept thinking to myself, "Ruth would be so pleased." Her doll is being designed and promoted just as she intended, as a vehicle for a child to pretend to be anything. Ruth would appreciate the emphasis on diversity and inclusion. She and her husband

Elliott were honored by the Urban League for their inclusive workforce. As Jewish people themselves, they knew about anti-Semitism, and abhorred discrimination.

I also had the chance to interview collectors and fans who live their personal creativity through the doll. You'll read about the man from Singapore who makes the most extraordinary Barbie clothes from tissue paper, and the young Australian girl who is a YouTube sensation for her live-action Barbie stories.

Ruth never imagined that Barbie would spark the imagination of all sorts of creators. Her genius was understanding the dreams of childhood. Dreams that we all carry into adult life, hoping to have them come true one day. I don't remember if I ever pretended that Barbie was a writer, but I always believed I could be anything. Perhaps Ruth's doll had something to do with that.

—Robin Gerber
Author

OPPOSITE: Mattel's 60th Anniversary doll released in 2019.

chapter 1

INSPIRING FANS SINCE 1959

There are endless ways to play with Barbie, and for sixty years, girls have loved the fantasies that the doll helps them create. Barbie lets them see themselves as women of action, women in the world doing interesting jobs and having amazing adventures. Girls see her as a blank slate that can reflect and embody their ideas about growing up and creating exciting futures to live into. And surely, if they have read the story of Barbie's "mom," the woman who first imagined the doll, they would want to play at being *her* as well. Barbie sparks inspiration likely because her creator, Ruth Handler, embodied it herself. In a 1994 book titled *The Story of Barbie*, author Kitturah Westenhouser asked this thought-provoking question that still intrigues fans and experts today:

"Is it the doll or her mother, Ruth Handler, who is *really* the legend?"

The idea of the doll that would become Barbie started in the early 1950s. Ruth Handler had an idea for a toy forming in her mind. This was unusual for her. She was usually busy running the day-to-day operations of Mattel as executive vice president, and was known for her skill at marketing and managing the young business—but not at creating toys.

Ruth spent her days making the hundreds of small and large decisions that kept Mattel growing. Behind a large wraparound desk—her black rotary phone on one side, an ashtray near her right hand—she ran the business side of Mattel. She had employees to hire and manage, products to inspect, budgets to approve, and a young family to tend to at home. Her life left little time for dreaming up new toys, yet an idea had flashed into her mind, and she had a strong feeling that it was a good one. This new idea was nothing like the popular toys that Mattel had become known for—like their burp guns and musical toys.

OPPOSITE: Ruth Handler, circa 1958, with several of Mattel's hit toys, including the Mousegetar, the Popeye Getar, and a few dozen Jack-in-the-Boxes.

Ruth was a person who followed her instincts. Diving into the competitive world of toy sales had been part instinct, part drive, and part good fortune.

It was a good time to be making toys in the United States. Soldiers had returned home after World War II ended in 1945, and they were eagerly starting families. Americans' standard of living had been rising as well, and that trend was continuing. Families had more money, and more leisure time to spend it. Ruth saw herself as a leader in growing a company that would fit in with parents' dreams of raising their children in a peaceful and carefree world.

Ruth focused on hiring the best and the brightest employees. Her detailed understanding of budgets and her extraordinary marketing sense had made her a recognized leader in an industry dominated by men. She knew she was far ahead of her time, as few women went into business after the war. But Ruth had an inner drive that left her unconcerned with what other women were doing. She knew what she had

ABOVE: Mattel Creations, which was incorporated in 1948, located in Culver City, California. Their office would later move to a larger location in Hawthorne, California.

to do, and though she loved her children, she once told a reporter that she could never be a stay-at-home mom.

Ruth had a secret weapon for Mattel's success: her husband, Elliot. He was a playful man with a love of toys and a wonderfully creative mind. The toys that launched Mattel had come from Elliot's fertile imagination and his skill at design. "You have to be able to spot trends," Ruth told a reporter in 1957. "My husband has a sixth sense. He's a great idea man." Research and design was Elliot's side of the business, while Ruth handled everything else. They had offices next to each other. People said there was "magic between them," both personally and in their work. Elliot said of Ruth, "She could do anything."

Elliot preferred drawing to engaging in conversation. He was known for sketching on tablecloths, napkins, or whatever was at hand. Throughout the 1950s, under Elliot's leadership, Mattel came out with the Mousegetar, the Musical Egg, the Musical Clock, a Bonneville racing

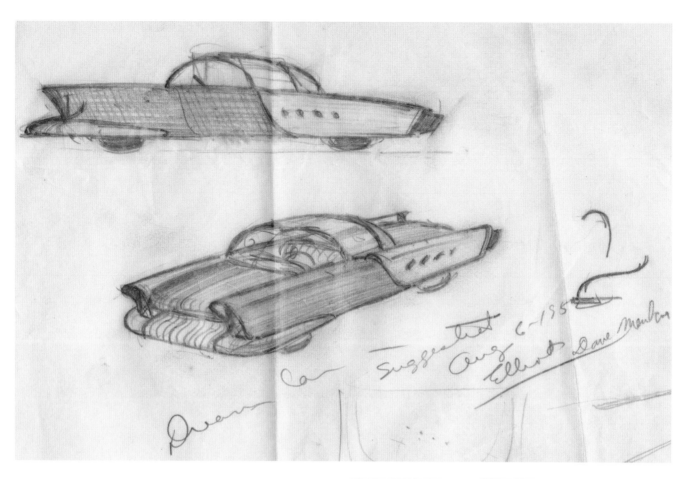

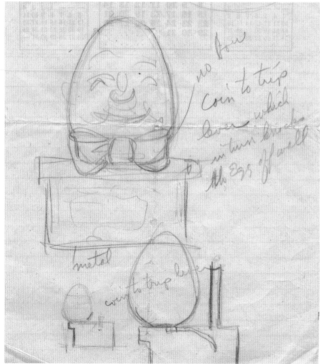

ABOVE: Original sketches from the 1950s by Elliott Handler, who was known to draft ideas on scratch paper, napkins, note paper, and anything he could use. Shown here are ideas for a Dream Car (top), Humpty Dumpty Rocker (bottom left), and the Hickory Dickory Clock (bottom right).

car, holster sets, Jack- and Popeye-in-the-Box, and more. On the strength of his innovative products, Ruth and Elliot had built a fast-growing toy company that was challenging its larger competitors: Kenner Products and Louis Marx and Company.

At a time when a woman needed her husband's approval to open a bank account, Ruth stood out as a boundary breaker. Elliot loved and admired her for her skills and determination. But her idea for a new toy tested his support, even as it broke boundaries that she had not imagined.

Ruth and Elliot had met as teenagers in Denver. He was the shy, quiet, brilliant artist. She started working at age twelve and was soon running the cash register at her sister's lunch counter. They met at a dance and were immediately drawn to each other. Little did they know that their storybook romance would lead to a business partnership that would exceed their wildest expectations and delight millions of people worldwide.

As Mattel grew, Elliot put together a large design team that had started to favor toy guns based on the popular cowboy shows of the 1950s. Elliot loved "cowboy stuff" and riding horses. He enjoyed going to the desert and chasing coyotes on horseback and taking the family to dude ranches, so toy guns were a natural extension of his personal interests. But it was the musical toys that grew from Elliot's boundless imagination that put Mattel on the toy-company map.

Mattel's first hit toy was a miniature ukulele, called the Uke-a-Doodle, which came to market in 1947. Elliot had designed it to look like the ukulele played by Arthur Godfrey, a popular radio and television star. The original Uke-a-Doodle was a plastic ukulele with steel strings and tunable pegs. In 1949, Mattel added a crank that turned to produce different children's tunes. Mattel's success with the toy ukulele led to a group of toys based on the unique mechanism designed by Elliot.

The mechanism Elliot had designed was a small box with tiny wires that were plucked when a crank was turned. The toys would play a variety of short tunes. The box could be inserted into any number of toys, from an organ grinder's musical barrel organ, to a hurdy-gurdy, to a Jack-

TOP: Ruth and Elliot Handler in 1941, with newborn daughter Barbara at five-and-a-half weeks old. BOTTOM: An advertisement from the 1949 Mattel Creations catalog for the Uke-a-Doodle Music Box, which was two toys in one: a child-size ukulele that also came with a music box that played popular tunes with the turn of its handle.

Chromatically tuned with real jet black keys that actually play

Futurland GRAND

Dimensions
Width: 8½ inches
Length: 11½ inches
Height Overall: 7¼ inches

Futurland GRAND

Attractions:

★ 17 Plastic keys
★ Real sharps and flats
★ Chromatically tuned
★ New type, patented Sound Board
★ Feather touch action
★ Colorful two-tone variegated plastic

An all-year musical toy favorite... the musical toy with 17 plastic keys, 10 white and 7 jet black keys that actually play... the only table model toy piano that has sharps and flats. Fabricated of sturdy washable molded plastic in bright toy-tested colors... Futurland toys have always been leaders in sales, profits and consumer acceptance. Amazingly low priced for volume turnover.

Write for prices and information

No. 412... Packed 1 dozen to a carton. Shipping weight 20 lbs. per carton.
Terms: 2% 10 days E. O. M., F. O. B. Culver City. Regular trade discounts.
Newspaper mats available.

TOP: Ruth and Elliott Handler in 1951 modeling some of their popular toys. **BOTTOM LEFT:** An advertisement from the 1951 Mattel Creations catalog for the Futurland Grand Piano. **BOTTOM RIGHT:** A group of three Mattel plant workers in the 1950s.

in-the-box. Over the next very profitable years, the same music mechanism was put inside several toys, including musical books. Within two years, the music box toys had brought in nearly nine million dollars.

There was one toy genre that Mattel had not fully entered: dolls. Mattel had created a small baby crib and baby doll in the late 1940s, and also had created doll *furniture*. But they had not yet created anything like the fashion doll that Ruth had in mind. Ruth and Elliot always looked for new toy ideas that were unique. Their originality and rigorous, precise production techniques were the special combination that had brought them far in just a short time within the toy industry.

The mainstay doll for girls in the 1950s was the baby doll. World War II had ended in 1945, and soldiers had returned from the Pacific and European battlegrounds anxious to marry, obtain civilian employment, and start families. Many women had worked at traditionally male jobs during the war, but they returned home to run their households and raise their children.

Mothers took care of babies, while fathers went off to work. Little girls were given baby dolls so they could play at what they saw in their own homes: cloth diapers that went in diaper pails for later cleaning, because disposable diapers didn't yet exist; glass baby bottles needing thorough sanitizing; and clothes-washing sets for growing families that included gear for line drying. Little girls watched the household work and cuddled their own Snookie, Plassie,

ABOVE: Ruth Handler watches as her husband and founder of Mattel, Elliot Handler, interacts with the popular Jack-in-the-Box toy, in 1960.

and Tiny Tears—all baby dolls for girls to play at one thing: being mothers.

But Ruth saw something in her home that she felt sure other toy makers had missed. In the book *Dream Doll: The Ruth Handler Story*, Ruth says, "It dawned on me that this was a basic, much-needed play pattern that had never before been offered by the doll industry to little girls." Her daughter Barbara loved to play with paper dolls. Whether it was more about role-play or fashion play, she liked the mature paper dolls—and the fashions that accompanied them. When Ruth took Barbara to the five-and-dime store on a Saturday afternoon, the young girl went right to the paper dolls. Barbara particularly liked color cutouts of Tillie the Toiler and others like her. Tillie had several fashionable outfits in her paper wardrobe. And there were many other adult paper dolls to choose from.

There were paper dolls of Hollywood stars, like Elizabeth Taylor and Debbie Reynolds; Teen Time and Teenager paper dolls; and bridal party, colonial, and comic-book character paper dolls. The girls could play at being adults or teens with these cutouts. They could act out roles, and they could pretend in a way that was impractical with baby dolls.

ABOVE: Ruth Handler in the 1960s with the Uke-a-Doodle—a product endorsed by Arthur Godfrey, a popular ukulele artist of the time—and the Cheerful Tearful doll whose face changes from happy to sad when her arm is moved.

Ruth took notice. She knew from watching her own daughter that there was a gap in what little girls were looking for and what was offered on the market. She had also become a keen observer of children as Mattel grew. A routine part of Mattel's toy development was inviting children to the company to try out toys so that developers could understand how children would use the toys, and then take those ideas back to development, making tweaks and changes wherever necessary. After watching many of these sessions, Ruth had developed a concept she called "play value," which was a combination of both the attention and the time that a child would devote to a new toy.

After observing her daughter Barbara and her friends play with adult paper dolls for hours on end, Ruth was sure that her doll idea had great play value. The paper dolls were simply cardboard cutouts of women, often in underwear or a bathing suit, just begging to be dressed. These dolls had to be carefully popped out of their cardboard backgrounds, which could then be stood up in a cardboard stand. They came with pages of clothes that needed to be tediously cut out with scissors. Tabs jutted out from the clothes so that they could be folded and pressed down around the cardboard figures to stay on; however, the tabs worked poorly. Clothes rarely stayed on properly, and to add to the frustration, the tabs would often tear off, and then the clothes wouldn't stay on at all.

Despite all the frustrations of paper dolls, Barbara and her friends preferred them to three-dimensional baby dolls and other dolls on the market, such as Madame Alexander, Posie, and Dollikin, which represented older girls with babyish faces. Madame Alexander dolls wore elaborate dresses and were treated more as collectibles than dolls made for active play. Dollikin might wear a fur stole and pearl earrings, but she still looked prepubescent.

As she watched her daughter playing with her friends, Ruth realized they wanted more than these dolls, which were an unrealistic hybrid between babies and teens. Young girls were searching for a way to play at the reality they observed in the adult world—to play out their dreams.

Ruth listened as the girls imitated adults, acting out what they saw at home and school, speaking in grown-

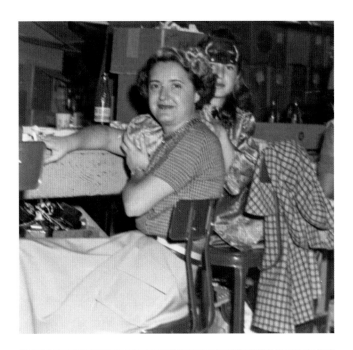

TOP: Ruth Handler with daughter Barbara. **BOTTOM**: An example of popular paper dolls of the time, Mopsy Modes paper dolls were modeled after the *Mopsy* comic strip, created in 1939 by Gladys Parker, who was both a cartoonist and fashion designer. Gladys was able to expand her interest in fashion with concepts she created in a series of paper dolls.

ABOVE: Vintage illustration of High School Paper Dolls from 1940, first published by Merrill Publishing. Paper dolls and their interchangeable fashions were an inspiration in the creation of Barbie.

up voices and mimicking grown-up conversation. As she watched, Ruth wondered, *Why don't these girls have a real doll to act out these fantasies? How much richer would their play be if the doll they held was three-dimensional, with adult clothes on an adult figure?*

Ruth felt sure she could recreate her daughter's play pattern. She also felt that an adult doll for girls would be the kind of original entry into the doll market that fit Mattel's vision. "I decided," Ruth told *Good Housekeeping* in 1967, "that a doll with a teenage figure and lots of glorious, imaginative high-fashion clothes would be radically different, and would appeal to today's girls who grew up faster than they used to." Her characteristic optimism ensured her that it would sell. With her own background as a young girl who had been raised by her sister, and who had gone to work in the family store at twelve years old, Ruth may have felt a personal attachment to the simple idea that she used to explain her doll: "My whole philosophy was that through this doll girls could be anything they wanted to be." Ruth took her toy idea to

Elliot, who always believed in her, always supported her, and felt everything she did was just right. But this time, Elliot pushed back. Ideal Toys had the Little Miss Revlon doll on the market. Elliot thought this doll, with her babyish face, budding breasts, and high heels, was what Ruth had in mind. But sales of Little Miss Revlon, which had been a hit for years, had started to decline. Why would they enter that market just as interest was falling off? Elliot's research-and-design team agreed with him about Ruth's idea, but for a different reason. The twenty male engineers agreed on one thing: mothers will never buy their daughters an adult doll with breasts.

Elliot and his team urged Ruth to go back to running the company. After all, toy creation was not her area. While Ruth handled Mattel's overall budget, Elliot and his team were given the largest budget inside the company to develop toys. They were the "blue sky" boys, responsible for coming up with ideas. They felt that Ruth should stick to what she was good at, and they would go on creating toys in the hot new market of guns and rockets.

ABOVE: Walt Disney (center) with Ruth and Elliott Handler, and several members of the Disney team, circa 1955.

The research team had a major success to back up their rebuke to Ruth: the Burp Gun. Mattel had taken a huge risk by advertising the new Burp Gun. toy on television, a relatively new medium for promoting toys. In the early 1950s, toys were advertised in catalogs or other print media. Advertisements were aimed at parents, who decided what toys to buy for their children.

Ruth was willing to bet nearly the entire net worth of Mattel on television advertising. She saw the opportunity in gearing the ads directly toward children. No toy company had ever taken such a risk. But Ruth's strategy paid off

when the Burp Gun advertisements aired on the new hit television show *The Mickey Mouse Club*.

The Burp Gun, a child-size machine gun so named for the sound of its bursting caps, became a huge success. Soon came a Winchester rifle, a Colt .45, and other cowboy-themed guns, along with real leather holsters. Mattel's realistic manufacturing and new approach to marketing made the company a growing threat to other toy manufacturers. Dolls were a risky distraction, especially the one Ruth wanted to make.

Ruth listened to the men's arguments, but she knew

ABOVE: Ruth Handler assists Elliot assembling a two-stage plastic rocket next to a Number One Barbie.

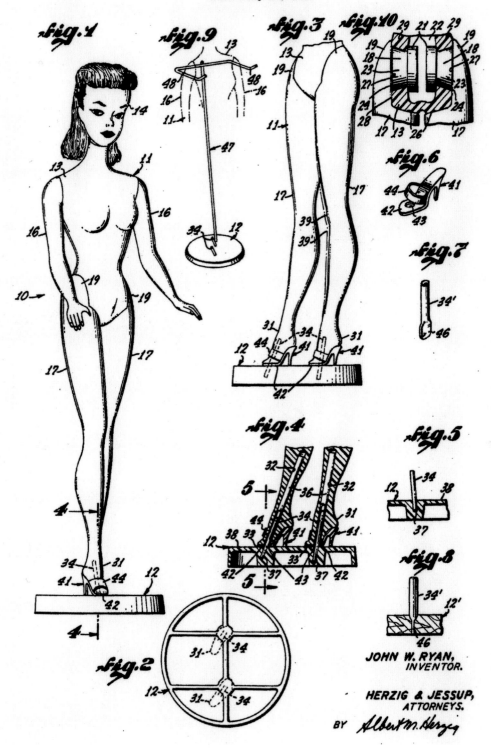

JOHN W. RYAN,
INVENTOR.

HERZIG & JESSUP,
ATTORNEYS.

BY Albert M. Herzig

ABOVE: The official U.S. patent for the "Doll Construction" of Barbie was filed on July 24, 1959, by Mattel's designer Jack W. Ryan.

#543

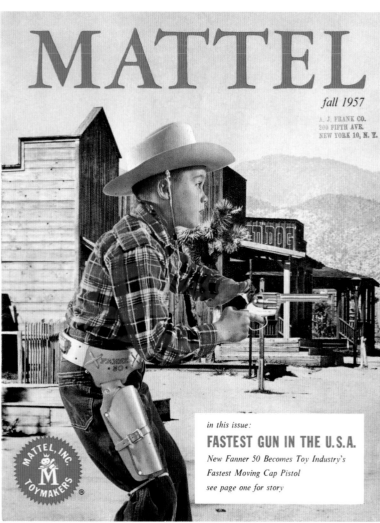

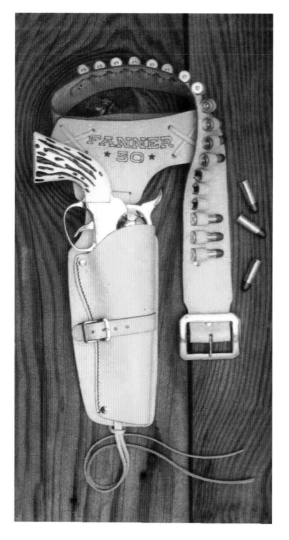

MATTEL FANNER-50

*PATENT NO. 2729011; OTHERS PENDING T.M.

MATTEL

fall 1957

A. J. FRANK CO.
200 FIFTH AVE.
NEW YORK 10, N. Y.

in this issue:

FASTEST GUN IN THE U.S.A.

*New Fanner 50 Becomes Toy Industry's
Fastest Moving Cap Pistol
see page one for story*

ABOVE: Mattel's Fanner 50 cap gun—a single-action with rotating cylinder—looked realistic, which was part of its success. Shown here are images from 1957, including an ad for the Fanner 50 (top), the cover of Mattel's Fall 1957 catalog featuring the Fanner 50 (bottom left), and the Fanner 50 inside its holster (bottom right).

they were wrong. Little girls wanted to play at being adult women, and adult women had breasts. For Ruth, the men's attitudes were not roadblocks, but instead drove her passion for her idea even further. Ruth didn't know the meaning of *impossible*. She was sure she would find a way to make her doll. She kept going back to the men, describing a doll with long legs, high-heeled feet, makeup, and nail polish. They said it would be too difficult and too costly to make. It would have to sell at too high a price point.

This was not the first time that Ruth had been told she couldn't do what she had in mind. Sarah, Ruth's older sister who raised her, had tried to stop Ruth from marrying Elliot. After two years of trying to separate them, Sarah finally gave up. Ruth was the kind of person whose determination grew when her dreams were denied. Just as she had persevered

to marry Elliot, she would hold on to her idea, believing she could make it work.

Meanwhile, thousands of miles away, in Germany, Reinhard Beuthien—a tall square-jawed man with a twinkle in his eye and a cigarette dangling from his lips—had just created a hit cartoon. Beuthien worked for a tabloid newspaper, *Bild-Zeitung*, which means "picture newspaper" in German, and the paper was true to its name. The editor asked Beuthien to come up with a cartoon to fill a space where a column had been pulled. Beuthien's first attempt featured a cherubic baby, but when his editor balked, Beuthien put the baby face onto the voluptuous body of a young woman and called her Lilli.

The reaction to Lilli was swift and enthusiastic. Soon Beuthien's Lilli was a hit across Germany. Taking advantage

ABOVE: Mattel designer Jack Ryan stands in front of a Fanner 50 display, circa 1957.

of his cartoon character's popularity, Beuthien teamed up with a toy designer to move Lilli off the page and to shape her into a three-dimensional doll. Although it was designed for adults, toy stores soon began carrying the buxom doll dressed in costumes ranging from a ski outfit to evening wear. As Ruth made plans for her family's first trip abroad, she had no idea that Lilli awaited her.

Aboard the great transatlantic cruise ship *Queen Mary* in July, 1956, Ruth and Elliot Handler—along with their two children—headed for a six-week tour of Europe. It had been several years since Ruth first proposed her adult doll. She had made many efforts to interest her toy designers, patiently explaining her vision of an adult doll with tasteful makeup, nail polish, hair that could be styled, and clothes— lots of realistic, well-made clothes. The American market had no such doll. Mattel could break new ground in the industry, she had argued.

The men listened with continued skepticism. Even if the doll might sell, she was told over and over again by her ten industrial engineers, the plastic molding available at that time would not allow for the detail she had in mind. Nothing like she described had ever been made, and the Mattel engineers were sure it would either fail or cost more than Ruth's demanding cost sheets would allow.

Perhaps Ruth thought about her doll, as well as the frustrating rejection she continued to face, as the grand ship, with its polished wood decks and beautiful art deco styling, sailed toward England's Southampton docks.

In an interview with author Kitturah Westenhouser for her book, *The Story of Barbie*, Ruth explains that after touring London and Paris, the Handlers stopped at the Grand National Hotel in Lucerne, Switzerland. The palatial hotel, sitting on the banks of Lake Lucerne, with views of the snow-capped mountains, must have seemed magical. More magical still was the surprise awaiting Ruth as she and Barbara went shopping in the quaint Swiss city. Approaching a local shop, they looked in the window to see a doll that captivated them both, but for different reasons.

They had found Lilli.

Barbara was surprised to see that Lilli looked like a realistic doll version of her adult paper dolls. Ruth saw

ABOVE: An original 1958 Lilli doll from Germany, shown here in her tennis outfit. Collectors are willing to pay thousands of dollars for an original in mint condition.

ABOVE: Shown here in a blue dress with white polka dots is a 1955 Lilli doll from Germany.

something far more surprising: her dream doll. Suddenly she knew that the doll she had envisioned *could* be manufactured, including its tiny details. And if the doll could be made for the overseas market, then surely she could get it made for consumers in the United States.

Ruth wanted to buy a Lilli doll and some clothing to go with it. But Lilli wasn't sold with separate clothes. If you wanted a different outfit, you had to buy the doll that wore that outfit. Ruth came to the conclusion that the razor-and-blade model would make much more sense. Let children get one doll, and they will buy lots of clothes to dress it.

Ruth must have been filled with ideas and excitement as the family sailed for home. Barbara adored her Lilli doll, and Ruth had gotten one for herself. In her interview with Kitturah Westenhouser, Ruth said, "I bought two of the dolls in Austria and gave one to Barb and took one for myself. When I went back to the factory I showed it to our people. I said this is what I have been talking about. The shape and

ABOVE: Mattel's success is owed to the innovation and design of their products. In the photos above, designers are hard at work at the Mattel headquarters, located in Hawthorne, CA, circa 1960s.

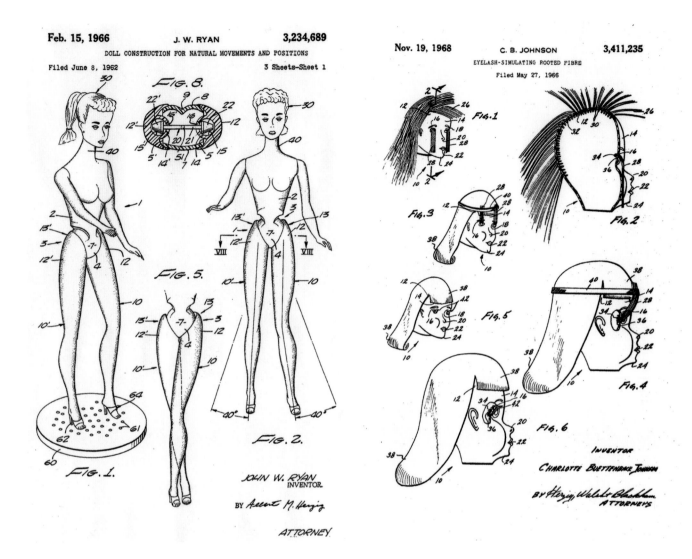

ABOVE: The original U.S. patents filed by designer Jack Ryan for Barbie's "Doll Construction for Natural Movements and Positions," invtented by John (Jack) Ryan and filed June 8, 1962 (left), and another for "Eyelash-Simulating Rooted Fibre," invented by Charlotte Johnson and filed on May 27, 1968 (right).

size, not the face or the clothes." She had the doll she had spent five years imagining, and she also had a plan.

Back at Mattel, Ruth showed the doll to their head of research and development, Jack Ryan, and to their production head, Seymour Adler, who hired an additional sculptor to work on the doll's face.

Ruth had found a close approximation of the doll she had been describing, and she told Jack to figure out how to make an original design. She estimated it would take about three years to get the doll to market.

Soon Jack was on his way to Japan to work on contracts for other toys, including wooden doll furniture that Elliot was designing. The doll furniture preceded Barbie by a year, and was built scaled down to accomodate dolls two

to three inches smaller than Barbie's 11½ inches. Ruth put Lilli in his hands, so that they could build furniture designed for the doll. She knew her design team would be winging it, but making a toy as original as the new doll always entailed a risk.

Mattel was just starting to manufacture in Japan because of lower labor costs, and Ruth knew that to make her doll marketable, she would need the savings that could be found overseas. But language barriers made communication difficult, especially for items that were as different as Ruth's doll. Jack had brought Frank Nakamura, a young, newly hired product designer, along to interpret. Frank had been hired by Elliot Handler when Mattel decided that they needed to move some production to Asia to save costs.

TOP: Ruth Handler and a Mattel sales representative meet with executives from Montgomery Ward, a department store retailer, in Chicago, 1959. **BOTTOM**: A Barbie sports a red dress while standing in the living room of her Barbie Dream House. The Dream House, which came with a kitchen, bedroom, and terrace, as well as "built-ins" and "pass-throughs," could be folded away compactly and came with a carrying handle.

A Japanese American with large eyeglasses and a bowtie, Frank spoke Japanese, which was critical to Mattel's new effort. He had come to Japan in 1957 to arrange the making of doll furniture for 8- to 11½-inch dolls. Now he returned to figure out how to make the doll itself.

Jack and Frank found one company willing to try to make the doll, but they struggled to explain the doll's details. Prototypes came out with eyes that were too exotic, and breasts that had the overly realistic addition of nipples, instead of the smooth surface that had been designed. The prototypes were sent back to Mattel headquarters, some of the rejects ending up in desk drawers. Years later, employees would chuckle over a Barbie torso, copper plated and covered with epoxy, that had the rejected nipples.

The Japanese engineers had their own problems. They labored to adjust the plastic molding so that every crevice was filled with the melted vinyl. Otherwise the doll might come out of the mold with no nose, or with odd bubbles on the body, or with brittle fingers that broke off.

The first stands for the doll were also a problem. The first-wave dolls had holes at the bottoms of the feet and shoes that fit over two metal prongs that stuck up from the bottom of the stand. The fit had to be exact, or the doll would fall over. If the doll were pressed down too hard, the leg might break off. Costly inspections were required, and the stand was abandoned in favor of a wire rack stand, and later a stand that held the doll under the arms. All of these decisions had to be considered while determining the price

ABOVE: Mattel hosts an open house for their City of Industry Facility, circa 1960s.

of the doll. Ruth wanted to keep the price low, knowing that she was selling a tiny mannequin whose clothing and accessories would bring the greatest financial reward.

Back at Mattel, Ruth had a big challenge to tackle: how to design and manufacture the doll's clothing. She set out to find the best fashion designer in Los Angeles. She wanted someone who understood more than apparel. They had to love color, pattern, and material, and they had to be precise, a perfectionist. Ruth—always aiming high—wanted realistic clothing right down to the snaps, buttons, belts, and zippers. Girls should feel like they were dressing a tiny person, a miniature embodiment of their future selves. She knew they would be captivated by the accessories. The precision of a tiny purse, a pearl headband, shoes, sandals, boots, sunglasses with tinted lenses, hats with a hint of a veil—all of these would hold children's attention and stimulate their play.

Ruth found her fashion queen at a social event.

Charlotte Johnson had been artistic since her childhood in Nebraska, where she was also a standout student. Tall and pretty, with a broad smile, Charlotte had been a clothing designer on New York's Seventh Avenue. When Ruth met her, Charlotte was teaching clothing design at the famed Chouinard Art Institute, where Walt Disney sent animators to be trained.

It's easy to imagine that Charlotte found Ruth's passion for her project irresistible. Ruth wanted "glorious, imaginative, high-fashion clothes." Charlotte taught during the day, but in the evening, Ruth would come to her apartment to talk about the doll's clothes. The two women tossed around thoughts about Ruth's ideas for a wardrobe of American clothes—exciting clothes for teenage girls that were tied to their activities, from prom dresses to wedding gowns to athletic and office clothing. Because the detail that Ruth demanded required labor-intensive work, Charlotte flew to Japan to arrange for

ABOVE: Mattel's design team pose with some of their popular products from the 1960s, including an original Barbie. Designers Charlotte Johnson and Jack Ryan sit at the table in the foreground.

Once again in 1960, Mattel made an outstanding impression. *Chatty Cathy*, the talking doll, stole the show. "She says eleven different things," was heard whenever two or more toy buyers exchanged information about what toys were "Hot." *Barbie* was spoken of as the most universally "sold out" doll in the country and the byword was to be sure and order enough dolls and costumes for 1960. In just two years, Mattel has become a leading factor in the doll field, accounting for more sales than many old time established doll manufacturers.

In musical toys, our Jacks, Ge-Tars and books are known as the top standards. . . . But this year there was an exciting newcomer, *Strum-Fun Getar*. Here again, buyers labelled the items "Hot."

Next to the government arsenal, ours is the largest in the country. All the guns — from the *Buckle Gun* to the *Winchester* and *Colt 6-Shooter Rifle* were branded as outstanding.

TOY SHOW

Before the Show, hours, days and weeks are spent by the Mattel home office group in pre-planning the "sell" for the year. Because of this pre-planning, we are the only toy company that can give each buyer an advance look at the advertising plan for the year. While the Sales Representative presents the line, he invites the buyer to see all the TV commercials that will be used during the coming year. Buyers are made aware of Mattel's half-hour show, "Matty's Funday Funnies" — which pre-sells 16,000,000 children every week, the year-round.

ЕACH year the Toy Fair "takes over" in New York City during the first week in March. Toy buyers from all over the United States and many foreign countries are invited to see the year's new toy lines. Competition for their attention is keen. The toy industry is unique in that few other industries attract so many ready-to-buy customers to one showcase event. Toy Show is a time for comparison, and to "get the feel" of a new toy. Here the buyers brand a new item as "Hot — A Good Standard — or a Stiff."

With the closing of the Fair, our Sales Representatives return to their individual territories — to begin the important function of holding jobber meetings. This year they are armed with a 30-minute filmed Mattel selling story featuring Clete Roberts, the noted news commentator, in a U.S. News and World Report production of "The Big News for 1960 — Mattel." Out of the planning and work come the orders which fill our production lines. Based on the results of the Toy Show, and the orders received since then, it looks like a very fine year ahead.

ABOVE: A 1960 advertorial demonstrating Mattel's success with many of their toys—including Barbie—at Toy Fair in New York City.

ABOVE: Ruth and Elliot Handler sit behind a collection of Barbie and Ken dolls, circa 1960.

the sewing to be done by the precise, yet less expensive, workers there.

In what must have seemed a great adventure for a woman from the Midwest, Charlotte ended up living in Japan for two years, creating twenty-two outfits for Barbie's first wardrobe. She lived in the famed Imperial Hotel in Tokyo, built in 1890 for foreign visitors, a short walk from the Imperial Palace. Charlotte's hotel room also served as her office, as she matched Ruth's drive with her own to build Barbie's first wardrobe.

Charlotte immersed herself in the Japanese garment trade, ordering specialty quality fabrics with small-enough designs to work for the miniature clothes. Having a sharp mind for business, she checked the fabric thread count to ensure it was as ordered. She would bring a magnifying lens to the fabric factory to inspect the material.

ABOVE: This 1960s Mattel advertisement shows a young girl cutting patterns from the Barbie and Midge Dressmaker, which allowed fans to create their own fashions and designs.

Charlotte designed perfect replicas of everything from lingerie to evening gowns. To ensure a perfect fit, she would start with a soft model of the doll, stick pins in it, and then take wax paper and form-fit it onto the doll, being sure it lay flat and unwrinkled. In this way, she made perfect patterns that children could easily slide onto Barbie's smooth body. Charlotte fought to keep Barbie's body uniform so clothes would fit throughout many years and generations of dolls.

She also trained a young Japanese woman named Nakamura Miyatsuka, who was in charge of inspecting the clothing. When Charlotte returned to the United States, it was Nakamura who was left in charge of the clothing production, which was a job that took her all throughout Japan.

Charlotte had taken on the unlikely job of wardrobe mistress for a doll. She could not have imagined how widespread and enduring her designs would become.

Ruth and Charlotte also worked together on the doll's look. Ruth felt the doll should not be "too beautiful," because she wanted girls to be comfortable with it, and not feel threatened. She wanted them to enjoy brushing the doll's hair, which meant rooting the strands in the head rather than simply gluing it to the scalp. She gave the doll shapely lips that were full, but not pouty. The eyes were black and white and glanced slightly to the

ABOVE: Three of Charlotte Johnson's original fashion designs for Barbie from 1959. Shown from left to right are Easter Parade, Commuter Set, and Gay Parisienne.

side, but not suggestive, although her eyebrows were arched. Her body was impossibly proportioned, but Ruth felt the doll's shape would enhance her clothes. And to show off the fashions, each of the doll's feet had a hole in the bottom so that the doll could be placed on her two-pronged posing stand, with the name *Barbie* etched in cursive on its surface.

As Ruth got her creation underway, her mind raced with ideas for naming the doll. Finally, she decided that, since her daughter Barbara had inspired her to dream up the doll, it seemed only fitting that the doll bear her name. The name Barbie was available, so the doll destined to be the most famous in the world got her name.

As the 1959 American Toy Fair in New York City approached, Ruth grew more and more apprehensive about selling Barbie. Along with the doll's clothes and a first line of furniture also being made in Japan, Mattel's

investment in Barbie was large. But the big toys being talked about for Toy Fair that year were guns and toy rockets that shot high up into the air. If any of the buyers knew about the Barbie doll, they mostly talked about it with the original skepticism that Ruth had encountered at Mattel. They did not believe mothers would buy their daughters a doll with breasts. Even Elliot was still skeptical. But nothing in marketing is more powerful than belief, and Ruth believed in Barbie. Even so, she thought about the Barbie doubters.

What if they were right? What if mothers rejected Barbie? She realized that she needed a special approach to marketing, a unique one to match her unique doll. She had heard about a man she thought could help her, but he was as controversial as Barbie, and he was in such high demand that he was difficult to hire.

His name was Ernest Dichter.

ABOVE: Ruth Handler stands next to a display for Barbie Boutique, which hosted examples of various Barbie products, circa 1960. **FOLLOWING**: Mattel's fashion designer, Charlotte Johnson, cuts fabric for a new Barbie design.

chapter 2

BARBIE GOES TO MARKET

There is a sixty-year history at Mattel of determining how best to market Barbie. Understanding and responding to parental concerns and getting public interest in Barbie were Ruth Handler's main concerns as she moved toward introducing the first Barbie to the world. She was a master at marketing, but she had never had a challenge like the doll she created.

It was 1958, and Ruth was almost into her third year of bringing the Barbie doll to market when she began to get seriously worried. Plans were being made for Toy Fair in March of 1959, where Ruth envisioned a grand unveiling of the doll. But the skeptics who had criticized her idea had grown louder and more numerous as the actual product was developed. Now they could see the body of the doll, and it was just what everyone had feared. Barbie had grown

from an idea into a too-realistic three-dimensional version of a full-grown woman.

The loud whispers of her doubters made Ruth think and rethink the key to every new product: marketing. Central to her plan was the man Ruth saw as an innovator like herself. He had a worldwide reputation, and provoked both strong praise and strong debate about his methods.

But once again, Ruth was ready to take a risk. She got in touch with Dr. Ernest Dichter and asked him to work for her.

Born in Vienna, Austria, Ernest looked every inch the academic researcher with his heavy-framed eyeglasses, pipe, and balding head. He held a doctorate in psychology from the University of Vienna and was a follower of Freud, but his ambitions took him far beyond any classroom. After fleeing the Nazis in 1938, Ernest landed in New York with

OPPOSITE: Mattel's original 1959 Barbie, dressed in her iconic black-and-white swimsuit and holding white sunglasses, complete with metal stand and original packaging.

a hundred dollars in his pocket and a bold idea for using psychoanalysis to revolutionize consumer marketing.

Ruth had already revolutionized the marketing of toys. Every year, more and more U.S. households had television sets, which were expensive, so usually there was only one. By the mid-1950s, the majority of Americans had a television in their home, and they watched together as families. The picture was black and white and required an antenna to get decent reception, but it mesmerized children anyway.

The baby boom after World War II led to children's programming on the growing medium. There were shows like *Sky King*, *The Howdy Doody Show*, *The Roy Rogers Show*, *Mr. Wizard*, *Romper Room*, and *Captain Kangaroo*, all of them airing on only four networks. Mattel had been advertising since 1955 on one of the most popular children's shows, *The Mickey Mouse Club*. This partnership was significant to Mattel. For the first time, a toy company advertised fifty-two weeks per year instead of the industry standard of four to six weeks leading up to Christmas time.

Mattel's first television ad for the Burp Gun had turned the tables on toy-buying in U.S. households. With ads featuring children—and aimed squarely at their point of view—Mattel had created dedicated consumers. Suddenly, children were begging for toys their parents knew nothing about. This opened the door for more direct toy marketing on shows, including whole cartoons or programs built around particular toys.

Even without the benefit of a consultant like Ernest, Mattel had devised commercials that spoke to children's fantasies. Mattel's first television ad for the Burp Gun does more than just show the toy and how to use it; a young boy stalks around the room, a Burp Gun at the ready, shooting at a projection on the wall of a charging elephant and imagining himself in "darkest Africa." The Burp Gun was marketed as part of a fantasy that thoroughly engaged children.

Touting a similar psychological focus, Ernest had sold his services to companies on the basis that they could sell products by connecting with consumers' unconscious feelings. After a stint with a market research company, he set up his own Institute for Motivational Research in

TOP: Ernest Dichter, American psychologist and marketing expert, was instrumental in working with Mattel's marketing team to ensure Barbie's success in the marketplace. BOTTOM: Ernest Dichter is shown observing customer shopping behavior during a tour of a supermarket in London on May 6, 1963.

a turreted mansion surrounded by heavy woods near the Hudson River in New York.

He set out to discover why people buy the way they do. He wanted to understand the entire person and their self-image. He believed people bought items based primarily on unconscious motivations and feelings.

In a large room over his garage, with a walkway surrounding a central stage, Ernest would ask consumers to play a role. He might ask them to act like a bowl of pudding or a bar of soap and then describe a product's personality, age, gender, and other characteristics. He walked around the stage, posing questions and taking notes. He saw it as a group therapy session, but about products. He called the sessions "psycho panels," and they were a method of determining consumers' desires that was as groundbreaking then as it is common today. He was holding the first focus groups.

Ernest also had a movie projector to show ads and record his focus groups' reactions. A big breakthrough came during his work for Betty Crocker. Consumers said they wanted foods that were easy to make at home, but they weren't buying them. Betty Crocker cake mix was the worst seller of this convenience product line.

As he would soon do with his Barbie research, Dichter brought together a group of wives and mothers, and let them free-associate about the cake mix. He realized that they felt guilty about the ease of the mix, even though they liked the convenience. They wanted the activity of baking the cake to be simple, but they also felt that they weren't doing *enough* for their families by only pouring the mix in a bowl and adding water. Ernest realized that the women needed a better sense of participation. He told Betty Crocker executives to rewrite the instructions on the box saying that an egg had to be added. Even though the mix didn't need

ABOVE: Ruth Handler is interviewed with Mattel's Getar on the set of KTTV in the early 1950s.

EXCLUSIVE! FASHION PATTERNS FOR *Barbie*®

TEEN AGE FASHION MODEL DOLL COSTUMES

Barbie fans will love 'em ... their mothers will too!

For the one and only Barbie Doll ... specially designed patterns by Advance Pattern Co., for an individual wardrobe of up-to-the-minute fashions. Six different Barbie patterns included in each of two envelopes, designed to fit Barbie's petite figure ... to a curve. Printed on pattern tissue.

Designed so simply that girls of all ages can cut and sew their own authentic Barbie costumes. Only ⅜ of a yard needed for each of 12 appealing, tiny outfits ... Casuals, Oriental Sheath, Dancing Frock, Kimono Lounger, Shorts for sports, Chilly Day Coats, Daytime Frocks, Evening Gown, etc. Entirely different designs than those Mattel offers as finished costumes.

the egg, Ernest's idea worked. Betty Crocker cake mixes became a huge success.

Ruth was fascinated with marketing and branding. She loved to learn about the latest thinking and methods. She probably knew that Ernest came up with the slogan "Put a tiger in your tank" for Exxon, a winning phrase that led drivers to equate gas with power. He was also famous for sending Chrysler sales soaring with his revelation that women made the family decision about car sales, so Chrysler should advertise in women's magazines. He also had ideas that seemed crazy, like comparing the "personalities" of oranges and grapefruits, finding the latter more refined. Ernest would soon validate one of Ruth's key instincts, that role play is an "important mechanism in maintaining emotional balance. Through role play, the child acts out fears, frustrations, aggressive tendencies, and insecurities." He went on to explain that a child's emotional health depended on both their ability to act out multiple roles and also the range of emotions that might go with them.

Ernest and his colleagues who used similar methods were called the "depth boys," and they promised to make corporations millions. Some people thought his theories were ridiculous. In 1957, Vance Packard wrote a best-selling book called *The Hidden Persuaders* that was deeply critical of his tactics. But by the time Ruth contacted him in 1958, Ernest had opened offices around the world and had a client list that ran to the hundreds.

ABOVE: An exclusive 1961 Mattel advertisement offers Barbie patterns specially designed for fans to create their own individual wardrobes, created by Advance Pattern Co.

ABOVE: This 1960s Mattel Family poster showcases members of the Barbie family, including Stacey, Brad, P.J., Casey, Julia, Christie, Tutti, Francie, Skipper, Barbie, and Ken.

Someday

The real world of little girls includes intimate friends like Alice and the Mad Hatter, Dr. Doolittle, Peter and Wendy, Pooh and Piglet, Dorothy and the Tin Woodman, The Little Prince, Beth and Jo and Amy and Meg.

A doll named Barbie® has become a part of this world. With her remarkable wardrobe of meticulously detailed fashions, she represents the glamour and delight of a grown-up world to millions of little girls. Their rich imagination makes Barbie very real, a portrait of themselves when they reach their teens. Barbie is someday.

Your child may see Mattel toys on one of our television programs. If she should ask for that toy, you can be confident of thoughtful originality and uncompromising quality. That quality is important to children ... and to us. Because ours is a most rewarding business. We make children happy.

ABOVE: Mattel's 1961 "Someday" advertisement featured a brunette Barbie dressed in bridal attire.

Ernest signed with Mattel because he was intrigued. He had never worked on a campaign for any toy, and this toy was definitely unusual. And Ruth's curiosity and desire to sell more toys went beyond her new doll.

At Toy Fair, Barbie would be competing with a realistic cartridge that shot small plastic bullets. The cartridge fit in a tiny derringer pistol, and a holster let the child activate the gun by puffing out his belly. Mattel had spent heavily to be sure the bullets would not fit any real gun, and Ruth wanted to protect that investment.

Mattel's toy rockets, popular because of the U.S. space program, were also getting a dangerous public reputation, although the company had come up with a safe, water-based propulsion system. Ruth wanted Ernest's research on these toys as well. She gave him an enormous contract for the time: $12,000.00.

Ernest set out first to find the "story" for Barbie that would get a positive and excited response from consumers and overcome any hesitation about her voluptuous body. He understood that the 1950s were a socially conservative time. Men's haircuts were short. Women mostly wore dresses, not pants. What story for Barbie would overcome the idea that she represented something foreign to the culture of the day?

Ernest used his well-developed focus group technique, which he had refined over nearly twenty years of work in the United States, as he explored the feelings of children and mothers about Barbie. He wanted them to reveal the personality of Barbie as they saw her. He let them free-associate about the doll, talking about whatever came into their heads. While mothers worried that Barbie was too sexual, girls saw an ideal. They loved her glamour and the

ABOVE: Barbie's Sew-Free Fashion-Fun by Mattel provided everything junior designers needed to create beautiful doll attire without sewing a stitch, 1965.

possibilities she presented. And mothers' mostly negative reactions softened when they examined the clothes. They were nearly as enthralled as the children were with the quality of the clothes and the potential for dressing the doll. And when one mother heard her daughter say, "She is so nicely groomed, Mommy," she decided the doll might encourage habits of good hygiene.

Mothers and fathers also saw the potential for doll play in much the same way they do today. A father told Ernest, "When my daughter was a little younger and used to play with dolls, there were many times that I could hear her talking to her doll and repeating word-for-word something

TOP: Five members of the Official Barbie Fan Club stand next to their collection. The girls in the photo were the one-thousandth Barbie Fan Club chapter located in Memphis, Tennessee. **BOTTOM**: Each member of the club received an Official Barbie Fan Club Membership Card like the one shown here.

her mother might have said to her. If she was feeding the doll, she would use the same words that had been used on her maybe an hour earlier. Playing with dolls gives a little girl a chance to be a perfect mimic."

A mother of six described the play of her three-year-old. "Claire's dolls are sometimes her friends and sometimes her children. Sometimes she loves them and sometimes she is very cross with them if they don't pick up their things, or she'll scold them for dirtying their clothes, or spank them for swearing. Then I hear myself . . . I must talk to her that way."

From these responses, Ernest presented Ruth with a plan to bridge the gap between mothers' views of Barbie and those of their daughters: present the doll with a persona as a teenage fashion model. Girls could enjoy the fantasy of a real adult with an enviable job. A fashion model would naturally have lots of clothes, and mothers could use the doll to help their daughters learn about looking well-dressed, groomed, and attractive.

Ruth loved Ernest's idea. She had always enjoyed nice clothing and makeup. From the beginning, her vision of Barbie had included lipstick, nail polish, and carefully drawn eyebrows. Barbie's original heavy mascara and striking lipstick reflected women's makeup of the day.

This was the kind of grooming that Ruth took care to do for herself. She also favored pearls, sometimes single-strand, sometimes multiple, sometimes chokers with stunning gemstones. Her hair was always styled, and like Barbie, her lipstick was bright red. And although Ruth was not long-legged and thin like her doll, she was buxom.

Ernest worked closely with Carson-Roberts, the firm creating Ruth's television ads. Together they gave Ruth what she wanted: an advertising campaign that matched the unique qualities she saw in Barbie. The first television ad for Barbie would break new ground in advertising and captivate little girls. But Ruth would suffer with her doubts for some time, worried the doll might not sell.

Carson-Roberts began planning the first Barbie television commercial, which was scheduled to air on *The Mickey Mouse Club* in the spring of 1959, and fully incorporated Ernest's findings.

Filming for the commercial relied on the most sophisticated equipment in the business. Hair stylists stood at the ready to do touch-ups, as if the doll were a real model. Barbie was posed over and over again as the producers tested her look. But the crew faced some unusual challenges, such as the dolls' tiny heads melting under the hot, intense lights. The solution? Freeze them overnight, and keep them in the freezer until filming started.

Barbie was treated as if she were a real person. The text and song for the ad use the word *doll* only one time. Instead, the camera pans across a number of Barbie dolls with ponytails and curly bangs in blonde and dark brown, staged for the production in a variety of outfits.

The advertisement ends with the camera closing in on a dark-haired Barbie at the top of a winding staircase, wearing a lace-covered wedding dress and veil, and holding a bouquet. Ruth was selling the fantasy not just of a dress-up doll, but of an adult world made for children's play.

In the commercial, the camera pans over the dolls while soft pop music plays in the background. The melodic, perky voice of a musician sings, "Barbie, you're beautiful. You make me feel my Barbie doll is really real. Barbie's small and so petite. Her clothes and figure look so neat. Her dancing

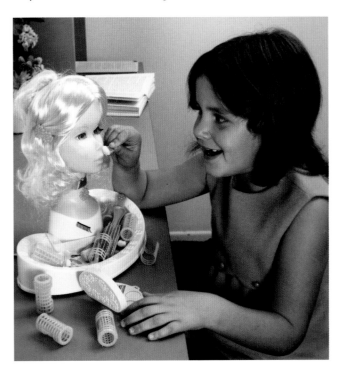

ABOVE: A young girl plays with Mattel's Barbie Beauty Center, released in 1972. The toy featured an almost life-sized head with rooted hair in the form of a ponytail that grows and grows. Accessories include rollers, bobby pins, a brush, a comb, barrettes, adhesive eyelashes, and cosmetics.

ABOVE: Mattel's Wedding Day Barbie, released in 1960, came dressed in a wedding gown and veil, holding a bridal bouquet.

outfit rings the bell. At parties she will cast a spell. Purse and hats and gloves galore, and all the gadgets gals adore."

A male narrator cuts in, "Barbie dressed for swim and fun is only three dollars. Her lovely fashions range from one to five dollars. Look for Barbie wherever dolls are sold." And then the singer continues, "Someday I'm gonna be exactly like you. 'Til then, I know exactly what I'll do. Barbie, beautiful Barbie, I'll make believe that I am you."

Ruth must have been pleased with the ad. It captured everything she envisioned about the doll and spoke to the main concern that might interfere with sales. Barbie was "beautiful" and "petite" and "neat," with "lovely fashions"— all qualities to both attract girls and make their mothers comfortable with a doll with breasts. When the ad was tested on girls, it captivated them. They wanted to pretend they were Barbie, or pretend that Barbie was whoever they wanted her to be. And they still do.

There is something magical for girls in holding a replica of a young woman, whether they see the doll as themselves at an older age or as a friend. Despite the objections to Barbie as being impossibly proportioned, girls simply see a toy that represents a way to enter the wider world.

Barbie is a wonderful prop. Girls use her alone, and also with friends and family, to cast the theater of their imaginative worlds. Barbie is a character that can morph into any of the many roles found written on her box— from a veterinarian to a fairy that flies and grants wishes. Why not? When a girl is handed Barbie, she's given the license to pretend, to live her own make-believe world that adults can enter, but only if they will play along. And that includes fathers.

Unlike the 1950s when gender roles were rigid, with women doing the parenting and men working long hours, fathers today play a bigger role in child-rearing. In the Mattel ad "Dads Play Barbie," a self-described football-loving dad plays the patient with one Barbie doll while his daughter uses another Barbie as the doctor. There is no mistaking the enjoyment both dad and daughter have as they pretend together.

Ruth did not imagine the colossal imaginative world her doll would create. She owned a toy company, and to grow

TOP: Mattel produced tiny book-like catalogues such as this 1961 issue of Barbie and Ken *Teen-Age Fashion Model*. **BOTTOM**: A close-up of the original 1959 Barbie. The handpainted heavy black eyeliner and highly arched eyebrows are trademarks of the Number One Barbie.

they needed new toys. Barbie was one of those, but much like the girls who would own her, Ruth had fallen for her doll. Despite the success of Mattel, the initial success of Barbie weighed on Ruth's mind.

By the time of Barbie's debut at Toy Fair on March 9, 1959, Ruth had grown Mattel to a $14 million company. It had been growing at 50 percent a year. There were three factories turning out sixteen different toys and a new factory being built. Ruth drove a pink Thunderbird, often with the top down. She dressed in sharp, well-fitted clothes and great accessories. And, like Barbie, she looked good in a bathing suit.

That's how the first Barbie doll came dressed. She was ready to be sold in a zebra-striped bathing suit, with black shoes, white sunglasses with blue lenses, and gold hoop earrings. The bathing suit was tailor-made with strechable

fabric that easily slid in place. She came packaged in a cardboard box with a cover announcing, "Barbie, Teen-Age Fashion Model," and drawings of the doll in different outfits. After all, how long could she be expected to stay in a bathing suit?

At a time when a new house cost $12,400, a family's yearly wages averaged $5,040, a gallon of gas was 30 cents, and a movie ticket was under a dollar, Barbie sold for $3.00, and her outfits ranged from $1.50 upward. And 1959 was a good time for a new toy. Unemployment had dropped to 5.5 percent, so parents were able to spend more. Television was becoming much more common in U.S. homes with shows like *Rawhide*, *Bonanza*, and *The Twilight Zone*. The country was growing, with Alaska added as the forty-ninth state and Hawaii as the fiftieth. And the Boeing 707 jet came into service, making it

ABOVE: From left to right, a vintage collection with Barbie Picnic Set (1959) with checked body blouse, clam digger jeans, straw hat, picnic basket, white straw cork-wedge shoes, and fishing gear; Barbie Q ensemble (1959) with rose sundress, white open-toed shoes, chef's hat, and apron that held cooking utensils; and the Resort Set, with red jacket, navy and white striped shirt, white cuffed shorts, white hat, and white vinyl cork-wedge shoes.

easier for Mattel's designers to travel to Japan and handle manufacturing issues with their new partners overseas.

Barbie came in a long, slim cardboard box, fit to her size. In later years, the box would expand to fit sets of Barbie with family and friends, along with clothes and accessories. In 2011, Mattel changed to sustainable packaging, but Barbie's box looked unchanged.

Inside the first Barbie box, girls found a small booklet advertising Barbie outfits and accessories. The outfits were sold as sets so that buyers got clothing and accessories together. The sets had names like "Cruise Stripes," "Suburban Shopper," "Commuter Set," and "Barbie-Q," which came with kitchen utensils. That first booklet advertised "Easter Parade," which came with a coat, purse, white gloves, pearl necklace and earrings, and shoes. "Picnic Set" included a hat with a tiny plastic frog and

flowers on the top, as well as a fishing pole with a sunfish on the hook. In this way, every set became a complete play opportunity as soon as it was opened. But there was a cautionary slip of paper in each doll box telling girls to "ease leg joints." This was to ensure the legs didn't snap when they were placed onto the small studs that fit into the holes in the bottom of the doll's feet. These features were new to the American toy market.

Mattel had multiple showrooms at the American International Toy Fair, but Ruth spent most of her time in the showroom for Barbie. Around the room, Barbie dolls were arrayed in various outfits and accessories on small stages or stairways that suggested they were in the middle of an activity. Ruth made sure every display was perfect. Every doll adjusted just right in her stand. Each spotlight showing off the dolls to their best advantage.

ABOVE: From left to right, a vintage collection with Barbie Suburban Shopper (1959) wearing a blue-and-white sundress, straw hat, and white open-toed heels, carrying a straw purse with fruit; Barbie Roman Holiday (1959) wearing the Cruise Stripes dress, a red-and-white striped coat, red straw hat, short white gloves, black open-toe heels; and Commuter Set Barbie (1959) wearing a navy cardigan suit and jacket, white satin body blouse, a red flower hat, short white gloves, crystal necklace, and navy open-toe heels, and carrying a red hatbox.

NEW! FAMOUS FASHION DOLL CASES— COMPLETE WITH DOLLS!

STANDARD PLASTIC PRODUCTS, INC.
A Subsidiary of Mattel, Inc.

NEW! BARBIE® CASE WITH DOLL #2000

- BARBIE Doll and Beautiful Vinyl Carrying Case Together
- Generous Storage Space for Doll and Clothing

Standard-leg BARBIE is fully visible in see-through window. Full color silk-screened all-around decoration on durable vinyl. 12¼" x 8½" x 2½". Doll in assorted hair colors. Hangers included. Std. Pack: 6/12 Doz.   Wt: 8 Lbs.

NEW!

SKIPPER® AND SKOOTER® CASE WITH SKIPPER #2001

- SKIPPER Doll and SKIPPER-Sized Vinyl Carrying Case
- Plenty of Storage for Doll and Clothing

Standard-leg SKIPPER is readily visible in clear vinyl window. Brightly decorated all around in silk-screened white polka dots on pink vinyl. 9¾" x 8" x 2½". Doll in assorted hair colors. Hangers included.
Std. Pack: 6/12 Doz.   Wt: 6¼ Lbs.

NEW! SKIPPER® AND SKOOTER® CASE WITH SKOOTER #2002

Same as above, except with standard-leg SKOOTER doll in assorted hair colors.

ABOVE: Mattel's 1966 advertisement for fashion doll cases—one for Barbie, and another for Skipper and Skooter—both of which come with a doll, and have space for storage, including hangers.

There were some glitches in the well-planned rollout of the doll. The manufacturer was late with the boxes to hold Barbie. Luckily, some samples were in the office, although they needed to be glued together by hand. Ruth fussed and worried, and then she waited for the buyers to arrive.

Mattel had a reputation for bringing innovative and popular toys to Toy Fair. Smaller manufacturers might wait impatiently for buyers to show up, but Mattel had to keep their rooms from getting too crowded.

Attendance was heavy at more than seven thousand people, up from the previous year. Shopping and sampling were brisk at the Sheraton-McAlpin and New Yorker hotels, along with the Statler-Hilton and permanent showrooms of manufacturers in the city. New toys included period dolls from Great Britain with real jewelry, a working soda fountain, a Dr. Seuss zoo, and a plastic infants' toy for the high chair or tub.

Although prices had not gone up from 1958, exhibitors noticed that more high-priced items were on display, and there was a trend toward quality merchandise. In addition, buyers wanted early delivery of toys because retail inventories were low. The stage was set for Mattel to have great sales, and Ruth hoped that Barbie would be part of the enthusiasm for buying.

As expected, many buyers showed up to see Barbie. Ruth had anticipated this strong reaction and ordered her Japanese suppliers to double production of dolls and clothes. But the initial enthusiasm of the buyers faded fast as they walked around the room. Three-quarters of the buyers walked out without placing an order, including the powerful buyer from Sears, Roebuck and Co. Just like Elliot and the Mattel research-and-design team, the toy buyers were skeptical that mothers would allow Barbie into their homes.

Ruth argued and cajoled over the three days of Toy Fair, but it was no use. Her orders weren't nearly enough to cover production. She was looking at a huge inventory backlog, and worse, the failure of her dream project. She wired Japan to cut production by 40 percent. Elliot found her later in their hotel and was shocked to see her crying. She had tried to prove herself as a toy creator, and she felt like a failure.

The months after Toy Fair did not look any better for Barbie's fate. Sales were slow. Inventory was backing up. The doll did not seem to be catching on with its intended audience, even though Mattel had taken the unprecedented step of sending displays for retail counters of Barbie dressed in different outfits. View-Masters, which allowed children to put in a disc and see pictures of Barbie in different clothes, were set up next to the displays. Ruth cut orders back more, trying not to end up with a glut of the doll.

But Ruth's tears and fears were premature. Those

TOP: A hostess checks the Barbie exhibition at the Toy Fair in Paris, France, February 4, 1967. BOTTOM: Skipper and Skooter trifold doll case from 1965, showing the interior of the case with Skooter and accessories.

singable commercials kept playing throughout the spring, and even though *The Mickey Mouse Club* was showing reruns in its final season, children were watching. When school let out, little girls knew what they wanted to play with over the summer. Barbie dolls started flying out of stores. Supply suddenly couldn't keep up with demand. Girls wanted more than one Barbie, which meant even more clothes. It took Mattel three years to catch up with the backlog of orders.

Opening a Barbie box was magical for girls. The feel of the doll was unique. After years of holding pudgy baby dolls, or fragile display dolls—some made of porcelain with delicate clothing—Barbie was sturdy. She could be held in one hand, even by a young girl. Her clothes were easy to get on and off, and play value came not only from imagining Barbie as a real woman performing various activities, but also looking at her tiny clothing catalog, and imagining her in different outfits.

The first true "fashion doll" had been born. Girls no longer saw dolls as their babies, but rather as themselves. A new kind of fantasy life had been unleashed for them, thanks to Ruth's vision. The doubters had asked, "How do you give a child a woman's body to play with?" Ruth had shown that Mattel trusted children to know what to do, and she had been proved right.

By the end of that year, 351,000 dolls had been sold, and a global icon had been born. Ruth felt thrilled when

ABOVE: A young girl named Debbie was the 500,000th member of the Official Barbie Fan Club, and her hometown welcomed her home.

ABOVE: Tracy Blanchette became Mattel's sweepstakes contest winner by being the one-millionth member of the Official Barbie Fan Club in 1965.

she would get on an airplane, or be out shopping, and see a child holding a Barbie. As she said, mothers and their daughters made Barbie a success. And Barbie had built Mattel's success. At the end of 1959, Mattel was about to add an enormous new facility to its growing manufacturing capability.

Ruth figured Barbie would sell for about three years, and then peter out like most toys. But Ruth's creation exceeded her wildest dreams. By 1965, Barbie had a fan club of more than six hundred thousand members, second only to Girl Scouts of the United States of America. Hundreds of thousands more joined clubs in Europe. By 1968, Ruth was a "lady millionaire," a "Woman of the Year," in the *Los Angeles Times*, and the well-known "mother" of Barbie.

Sixty years later, more than a billion Barbie dolls have been sold all over the globe, and sales top $1 billion annually. Barbie is one of the most popular toys ever, and you can find her in more than 150 countries.

Barbie also fueled huge growth for Mattel. By 1970, with Barbie and related products having brought in more than $600 million in revenue, Mattel was a global operation. Ruth visited her offices in Canada, Central and South America, Western Europe, Asia, and Australia. There were more than five million square feet of office, research, manufacturing, and warehouse space, and twenty thousand workers.

Over time, Barbie also became a sought-after collectible, along with her friends, family, clothing, and accessories. She has created hundreds of thousands of passionate followers worldwide who are sure that Barbie is forever.

In 2018, at the National Barbie Doll Collector Convention,

ABOVE: From left to right, a vintage collection with Barbie Winter Holiday (1959) dressed in hooded T-shirt, black footed leggings, white vinyl coat, red vinyl gloves, and carrying a plaid zippered bag; Barbie Cotton Casual (1959) wearing a navy-and-white striped sleeveless dress with an accent bows on the bodice, and white open-toe heels; and Barbie Peachy Fleecy (1959) with winter-white wool fleece coat, brown felt hat, brown open-toe heels, and carrying a mustard clutch.

Bradley Justice received a unique honor. Bradley was named "Barbie's Best Friend" for his work with *Doll News Magazine* and his research and preservation of the Barbie collection at the United Federation of Doll Clubs. The prestigious award is the only one given at the convention, and Bradley more than deserved it.

For Bradley, his love of Barbie started at five years old. "I first met Barbie in 1975," Bradley explains. "I spent the summer with my mom's side of the family in the eastern part of North Carolina, and my cousin Caroline had just gotten Sweet 16 Barbie. She had a trunk full of Barbie and Ken, and we played together with the dolls. I was smitten with Sweet 16, thought she was the most gorgeous thing I'd ever seen. After I went home, I asked for her, but I got Malibu Ken."

Despite his disappointment, young Bradley continued to be fascinated with Barbie. The next summer, his cousin gave him her older sister's Barbie—a twist-and-turn Stacey. After that he saved his five-dollar-per-week allowance to buy more Barbie dolls, along with clothing and accessories. He started making clothes, and he had endless adventures with Barbie in his backyard. His two brothers had other dolls popular at the time, like G.I. Joe and *Star Trek* characters. Bradley remembers many hours of making up stories that involved all the dolls, including his Barbie group. His Barbies were featured on *Gilligan's Island* or part of a pretend trip to the lake where Bradley would go with his cousins. Bradley says, "I always had this crazy imagination and would get frustrated with friends who didn't know how to play make-believe. That's what kids grasped from the first Barbie commercial—that Barbie was for playing make-believe, and they ran with it."

But at eleven years old, Bradley stopped playing and started collecting. He saw a program on television with Sybil DeWein, who wrote what is still considered the bible of Barbie collecting, *The Collectors Encyclopedia of Barbie Dolls and Collectibles*. DeWein was being interviewed because she had a vast collection of Barbie dolls, and she talked about how the first Barbie was worth hundreds of dollars.

After that, Bradley spent his weekends at garage sales or flea markets or anywhere he could find Barbie or her

ABOVE: Barbie is dressed in the Golden Girl attire, released in 1959, wearing the same sheath dress as seen in the Evening Splendor set, short white gloves, brown open-toe heels, and holding a turquoise corduroy purse.

clothes and accessories being sold at a discount. He could buy an item for five dollars that would be worth hundreds of times that amount. This was a fun and lucrative "job" for a teenager.

Throughout his teenage years, Bradley pursued his collecting passion. His father, who hadn't been thrilled with his initial interest in the doll, began to see the financial opportunity Bradley had created for himself. He saw that Barbie was a means to an end for his son and was very supportive. By the time college came along, Bradley had enough duplicates and triplicates to sell to pay for food, books, and other expenses at his community college and then later at North Carolina School of Textiles, where he graduated with a degree in merchandising and marketing.

After college, he worked as a buyer for a women's clothing store for nine years, but ever since, he's been a full-time collector.

Bradley explains that selecting Barbies in the early days of collecting was a kind of underground network. A lot of dealers did not acknowledge that Barbie was collectible, but then "the list" was created. In those pre-Internet days, you would send a dealer a self-addressed stamped envelope with a list of what you had and what you wanted. You bought by mail, which could take years. It took Bradley five years to find the Golden Glamour outfit from 1965, with its very detailed, complicated items, including a fur hat, long gloves, and spiked shoes. It is extremely rare.

Unlike today, where so much can be found on eBay, collecting was a mail-order business, or you had to sell at doll shows or conventions, where you could find other people who loved Barbie.

Bradley says his greatest find in collecting has been all of the friendships he's made. He also happens to have a great story of a Number Three Barbie he found at a thrift store for a dollar. It was in pristine condition, with great skin tone and perfect hair—the kind of find that makes a collector very happy.

What is so fascinating about the first editions of Barbie? Bradley explains that they represent "fashion in miniature." Everything about them was new. "With Barbie, nothing

ABOVE: The original 1959 Number One Barbie, with black-and-white zebra-striped strapless swimsuit and black open-toe heels, is one of the most sought-after dolls in the Barbie collection.

had existed before," Bradley explains. "Everything had to be created for her. People were fascinated with her being miniature and tiny, but also with the glamour and detail. You wanted everything about Barbie, which was why she was destined to create a collector culture."

Bradley calls himself a "catch-and-release" collector. He loves the thrill of hunting for a doll or various Barbie-related items, and then he's ready to let them go. But there are people who want it *all*, who want everything about Barbie. Bradley explains, "Barbie speaks to them, and they want to be able to see everything about her all together as one collection. There are also some people who just want what they had as a child. Some want Barbie for art. They love things like the sequined Bob Mackie gowns. Each doll, each fashion tells a story of design, creation, marketing, and delivery."

Bradley says having the first is like having the face that launched a thousand ships. "She's ground zero, the original, the one that started it all." Very soon after those first dolls went to market, Mattel started changing things about Barbie. But collectors love the arched eyebrows and vampish look, which changed early on.

Bradley has done more than collect. He was also the Region 8 director for the United Federation of Doll Clubs and curator for the Doll and Miniature Museum of High Point, North Carolina. Although as a North Carolinian he loves antique French fashion dolls and cloth dolls, his passion is still Barbie. He has curated three museum exhibits of Barbie and is a tireless researcher of Barbie history and particularly Charlotte Johnson, Barbie's first clothing designer. No wonder he was named "Barbie's Best Friend."

Bradley thinks Barbie will always be around because there's never been a doll created with the amount of attention that she receives. "She's monumental, cultural, iconic, and generations have played with her, including grandmothers, mothers, daughters, and sons. Each generation approaches Barbie a little bit differently, and each play pattern is a little different, because children's lives change with the times. But Barbie will always be there with them."

ABOVE: Barbie is shown wearing the yellow Sweet Dreams outfit from 1959. **FOLLOWING**: The millionth Barbie doll arrives in Germany, 1965.

chapter 3

BREAKING BOUNDARIES

Barbie started out as a teenage fashion model, but she has come a long way from that first job, and she still has a long way to go. Barbie "careers" have reflected not only the broad range of women's roles in the world, but also their aspirations. She has also gone beyond early expectations of how children would play with her.

In 1963, the *Saturday Evening Post* wrote, "Mattel has proved that girls in the nine to thirteen age group want a doll not to mother but as a means of looking ahead to the days of the pizza party, the football weekend, and the Junior Prom." That view of girls' dreams and imaginations was far too narrow. Even in the 1960s, girls wrote in with questions like, "Why doesn't Barbie have a parachuting outfit?" Ruth was listening, and Mattel responded. The runway may have been where Barbie took her first steps, but by 1965 she had been a fashion editor, singer, executive ("career girl"), student teacher, and astronaut.

Barbie became an astronaut before the first American woman astronaut, Sally Ride, went into space. Ride joined NASA in 1978, but she didn't join the crew of the space shuttle *Challenger* until 1983. Astronaut Barbie also went to the moon four years before American Neil Armstrong took his amazing walk and said the famous words, "That's one small step for a man, one giant leap for mankind."

Barbie won an Olympic gold medal not long after the 1972 Olympics in Munich. She also had the courage to become a surgeon at a time when the total number of women physicians in the United States was around 5 percent.

In the 1980s, when the number of women veterinarians had begun to increase, Barbie took up the profession. And thanks to the growing popularity of music videos, Barbie dolls often took on the job of rock star, although she had been a star to little girls since she first came on the market.

The 1990s were a breakout decade for Barbie. In 1992,

OPPOSITE: A young French girl poses in 1965 with her new Christmas toys: Miss Astronaut Barbie and Mr. Astronaut Ken, ready for their journey in space.

Americans elected more women to Congress than ever before. It was the "Year of the Woman," and Barbie kept up with modern culture by entering a number of careers that had traditionally been reserved for men. At the beginning of the decade, Barbie became a naval petty officer, with a crisp white uniform and sailor's tie.

Barbie served in many other military roles, from medic to pilot to officer. She became an Air Force fighter pilot in 1991, two years before Jeannie Marie Leavitt achieved that goal.

In the actual Year of the Woman, 1992, Barbie became a Marine Corps sergeant, a business executive, and most notably, a candidate for President of the United States. Not only had there never been a woman president at that time, there had not even been a woman candidate from a major party on the ballot.

In 1993, Barbie became an army medic and a police officer. Two years later, she was a firefighter in a bright yellow uniform, although less than 2 percent of firefighters in the United States were women at that time. Before the decade closed, Barbie entered two more nontraditional jobs, becoming a dentist and a commercial airline pilot. She also became a Major League Baseball player in 1998. To date there are no women who have had that job—but Barbie has always been ahead of her time!

ABOVE: From left to right, a collection showing some of Barbie's many careers, such as Astronaut Barbie (1965) wearing a silver spacesuit, white helmet, and brown boots; Surgeon Barbie (1973) wearing light blue scrubs, a face mask, cap, and stethoscope, and holding a towel; and Rockstar Barbie (1986) wearing a hot pink jacket with matching leggings, a pink and silver dress, and white boots, holding a white microphone.

In 2004, Barbie again ran for president, this time in a television-ready, apple-red pantsuit. The 2000s saw Barbie caring for babies as a neonatal doctor, dancing as a ballerina, and coaching her soccer team.

Most recently, she's broken new ground again as an architect, a race car driver, and a computer engineer. And in a third election campaign, Barbie ran for president in 2012, wearing a signature pink jacket with matching skirt.

Of course, from the very beginning, before Barbie was even brought to market, girls understood that she could be anything they imagined, including figures in their own lives. In the focus groups run by Ernest Dichter,

the psychologist Ruth hired to determine how to market Barbie, girls gave their reactions.

One eleven-year-old named Judy said, "Oh, she's a teenager." Another girl, Sharen, said, "Mine is a business woman. See the navy suit and the flower hat? She is going out to dinner and maybe dancing afterwards. Doesn't she look smooth?" Carol responded, "Mine is a debutante. See, she is all dressed up to go to a ball. She even has a little mink hat for her head. Doesn't she look darling?" And Patricia chimed in with, "Mine is a bridesmaid. She is going to Mass. See, she has on this pretty pink dress. She is all dressed up for church."

ABOVE: From left to right, a collection of Barbie's careers continues with Army Medic Barbie (1993) wearing full camouflage, and a red beret, and holding two green army bags; President Barbie (2004) dressed in a red pantsuit, and a scarf, and carrying a black bag; and Architect Barbie (2011) wearing a blue ombre dress with hot pink trim, a black jacket, black boots, glasses, and white hard hat, and holding a document-carrying tube for blueprints.

thank you for
Raising your
voice! — ♡ The Barbie
Team

09.16.15

In another group, an eight-year-old said, "I like her. She looks pretty. I could pretend she was going out to dinner, or going on a trip for the summer and afterwards going to college, and the years pass and she gets married. I could pretend she was going to the library to get out books, and I was the librarian showing her around."

This girl went on to explain what must have been a sad experience for her or someone she knew, showing Barbie's potential from the beginning to help children deal with their emotional life. "She could be going on a honeymoon. Her husband has a big boat . . . They go to the country, play ball . . . They went swimming . . . She got pregnant. She got sick and after the baby was due, in a week, the baby died. They had to take the baby away."

This early research into how children reacted to Barbie has informed the brand's evolution over six decades. This is especially true today, when Mattel is laser-focused on Barbie as a grand canvas on which girls can paint their dreams. Today's massive surveys help Mattel understand what consumers prefer, and their thinking about a new toy. For instance, the Barbie line of inspirational dolls involved asking 80,000 mothers worldwide about what they would like to see in a doll, and what their concerns were for their daughters.

ABOVE: The Zendaya Barbie (2015), created in the likeness of Zendaya Coleman—a singer, actress, dancer, and model. Michelle Chidoni, a spokesperson for Mattel, said of Zendaya, "She's a role model who is focused on standing up for yourself, your culture, and for what you believe in—that's very relevant for girls."

ABOVE: A collection of posters from Mattel's 1999 Barbie campaign designed to inspire and empower girls.

A whopping 86 percent worried about the role models that their daughters saw around them. The Inspirational Barbie dolls address mothers' concerns, and generate publicity each time one is introduced. They also influence the culture, getting the media, commentators and consumers talking about great women both today and in the past. And that's all before girls start playing with them!

In 2015, Barbie designers came up with an exceptional group of Shero Barbie dolls, which included famed director Ava DuVernay, who directed the film *Selma*, and Olympic fencer Ibtihaj Muhammad. In 2018, Mattel expanded the Shero group with "Inspirational Women," a fascinating group of Barbie dolls—such as the actress, singer, and dancer Zendaya Coleman—that arrived in time for International Women's Day on March 8. The new Barbie dolls represented the largest lineup of role models in the doll's history. As Mattel put it, "You can't be what you can't see."

What makes a Shero, or inspirational woman? There are many answers to that question, but the women chosen to be portrayed as Barbie dolls share a positive attitude, passion for their jobs, courage, an interest in helping other people, and a strong work ethic. They are women who respect others, who are willing to speak up, take risks, and be brave and generous, and who step forward to lead.

These dolls answer parents' concerns about having great role models for their daughters. As Ruth first determined in the 1950s, girls want the chance to act out their dreams of adult life. What better toys to do that with than this new group of accomplished, diverse, and inspiring women?

Here are some of the Inspirational Women:

Patty Jenkins is a dynamic, award-winning film director, best known for the blockbuster hit *Wonder Woman*, which was the highest grossing film of the summer and the third-highest of the year in 2017. Mattel modeled a Barbie doll after her, complete with a camera.

Chloe Kim is an American snowboarding champion. In the 2018 Winter Olympics, she became the youngest woman to win an Olympic snowboarding medal when she won the gold at only seventeen years old in the women's

ABOVE: "Become Your Own Hero" poster from Mattel's 1999 Barbie campaign designed to inspire and empower girls.

snowboard halfpipe. The Barbie doll modeled after her comes dressed in a yellow jacket and camouflage snowgear, and equipped a white snowboard.

Get inspired to protect the environment with Bindi Irwin, a star on Australian television and a talented singer and dancer, who is also a committed conservationist. She had a documentary on Discovery Channel called *Bindi the Jungle Girl*, and was a champion on *Dancing with the Stars*. Mattel created a Bindi Irwin doll dressed in khakis and accompanied by a friendly koala hugging her arm.

Go for the knockout with Nicola Adams, a British boxing champion in the flyweight division, and the first woman to win an Olympic medal for boxing. After winning two gold medals, she was awarded an Order of the British Empire (OBE), the highest honor her country can give. And Mattel awarded her with the honor of creating a doll in her likeness, wearing a black-and-white training jacket and sporting an ultra-cool hairstyle.

Ride the wind with Çağla Kubat, a champion windsurfer and sailor from Turkey. She has a degree in mechanical engineering and has also been a model and an actress. The doll modeled after her comes dressed in a pink and blue wet suit, ready to take on the waves.

Get cooking with Hélène Darroze, a French chef, who has not one, but two Michelin stars for her three restaurants. She's a fourth-generation chef who loves to bring people pleasure through food. She's also a knight, admitted to the French Legion of Honor in 2012. Her doll comes dressed in a stylish crisp white double-breasted chef's coat.

Spike the ball with Hui Ruoqi, a volleyball champion from China. She started playing in elementary school and was part of the team that won Olympic Gold in 2016. She has a shelf full of medals, which also include a silver medal from the 2014 World Championships, a bronze medal from the 2011 Japan World Cup, and two gold medals from the Asian Championship. Sporting a perky ponytail, her doll comes dressed in a white tank top and red shorts, and she carries a yellow and blue soccer ball as an accessory.

Knitting her way to the top is Leyla Piedayesh, an Iranian-born German fashion designer and entrepreneur.

ABOVE: A Shero Barbie in the likeness of Boxing Champion Nicola Adams, released in 2018, wearing black-and-white shorts and training jacket with gold trim, white high tops, and white boxing gloves.

She was first inspired by a pair of knitted wrist warmers she found at a flea market. She began knitting her own creations and now owns the wildly popular fashion label Lala Berlin. Her doll has long brown curly locks and comes dressed in a fresh yellow pantsuit.

Hit the long drive with Lorena Ochoa, a professional golfer who caught the world's attention. At eleven years old, she knew she wanted to be the best in the world. She achieved her goal, as well as a place in the World Golf Hall of Fame. She was the top-ranked female golfer for 158 consecutive weeks and the first Mexican golfer to be ranked number one in the world. Her doll is wearing a white cap, purple collared golf shirt, and classic golf skirt. She comes carrying a golf club.

Travel around the world with Martyna Wojciechowska, Editor in Chief of *National Geographic Poland*. Known for writing about her world travels, she's climbed the highest mountains on all seven continents. Fittingly, her Polish television show is called *Woman at the Edge of the World*. Her doll is dressed in smart black pants and top, accented with a sassy pale green jacket.

Go for the goal with Sara Gama, a soccer player from Italy, where she plays defender for the national team. She was the team captain in the 2008 European Championship, and her team won. Her doll comes dressed in a black-and-white Jeep soccer jersey, white shorts, and white knee-high socks.

A star of the big screen, Xiaotong Guan was born into an acting family and has been a star in movies and television in her native China since she was a child. She is known for her roles in the films *Nuan*, *The Promise*, and *The Left Ear*, and the television series *To Be a Better Man*. In 2017, she became the ambassador for "World Life Day," a joint campaign by the United Nations Environment Programme, International Fund for Animal Welfare, and The Nature Conservancy. Her doll comes dressed in a white sheer top over a sundress, and carrying two miniature Barbie dolls of her own.

Yuan Tan is the prima ballerina of the San Francisco Ballet. She is known as the greatest Chinese ballerina of all time and has danced the lead in several major ballets. This

ABOVE: The Gabby Douglas Barbie doll, released in 2018, celebrates the accomplishments of this extraordinary gymnast and role model, dressed in a pink and black Nike tracksuit over a stars-and-stripes leotard.

ABOVE: Three dolls from the 2017 Barbie Inspiring Women Series paying tribute to the incredible heroines of their time, including (from left to right) aviation hero Amelia Earhart, artist Frida Kahlo, and NASA mathematician Katherine Johnson.

critically acclaimed dancer's doll comes dressed in a frilly white tutu and wears a sparkly tiara.

Vicky Martín Berrocal is a Spanish fashion designer, businesswoman, and television personality with a popular line of bridal and party dresses. Featured in Mattel's #MoreRoleModels social media campaign, her doll comes wearing a pink and blue dress, with her hair pulled back in a low, neat ponytail.

Amelia Earhart was the first woman to fly solo across the Atlantic Ocean. In 1923 she received the sixteenth international pilot's license ever issued to a woman, and went on to set many flying records and write best-selling books. She even started a line of pilot-inspired clothes that was advertised in *Vogue* magazine. When she flew into the sky at night, she described the stars as seeming "near enough to touch." Her doll comes dressed in a brown bomber jacket, bodysuit, scarf, goggles, and a helmet—ready for takeoff!

Paint the world with Frida Kahlo, a Mexican artist who painted haunting self-portraits and vivid, imaginative flowers, influencing an entire generation of artists. She described herself as a child who went around "in a world of colors." She loved to look dramatic, wearing arresting colors and putting bright flowers in her black hair. Her doll comes dressed in a long traditional Mexican dress, a fringed red shawl, and a floral headpiece.

Number the stars with Katherine Johnson, a NASA mathematician and physicist and one of the first African-American women to work on the complex mathematical equations that led to space flight. She started high school at ten years old, going on to be one of the great mathematicians of her day. When NASA switched to computers, they had Katherine double-check the accuracy of the results. Katherine's story drove the hit movie *Hidden Figures*. Her doll comes wearing a collared pink dress with pleats and belt, stylish glasses, and a NASA name badge.

Ibtihaj Muhammad is an American sabre fencer and a member of the United States fencing team. In 2016, she won a bronze medal in the Rio de Janeiro games, becoming the first female Muslim American athlete to earn an Olympic medal. Her doll is dressed in a white fencing outfit, including

her hijab and her fencing mask, and is accessorized by a silver-handled fencing sabre.

Ashley Graham, an American model and body activist, is hailed for breaking stereotypes and is known for her accessibility and body confidence. She celebrates what real women's bodies look like rather than standards set by the media and fashion industry, and has been described as an "ambassador of the real beauty movement." Her curvy doll comes dressed wearing a sparkly black dress with a denim jacket.

Misty Copeland, an acclaimed prima ballerina, was considered a child prodigy who quickly rose among

ABOVE: Model and activist Adwoa Aboah poses with her new Shero Barbie doll made in her image, released March 6, 2019.

the ranks and became the first African-American to be appointed to principal dancer. She loves giving back and has worked with many charitable organizations dedicating to mentoring young people. In 2015, she was named one of *Time* magazine's "100 Most Influential People." Her doll comes dressed in a striking red bodysuit and tutu, with red toulle hairpiece.

American film director, writer, and producer Ava Duvernay became the first African American female director to receive nominations for both a Golden Globe and an Academy Award for Best Picture. In 2016, she directed an Oscar-nominated documentary about the criminalization of African Amercians and the U.S. prison system. Her doll

comes with long, braided hair, and is wearing a sleek black outfit, charm bracelet, and white heels.

Mental health activist and model Adwoah Aboah is one of the most recent inspirational women recognized by Mattel with her own Shero Barbie. On her public Instagram account, Aboah writes, "My very own Barbie! It's mad! Seeing my own doll that has my skin color, shaved head, freckles, and my tattoos is beyond mad. I spent the majority of my childhood wishing for blonde hair, pining over Barbie's light skin and blue eyes. All those years ago and I didn't feel like I was represented anywhere. But today with my big toothy grin, I feel so very proud to have been awarded this Shero doll for all the hard work I have put into

---

ABOVE: (From left to right) The Barbie Look: Lace Dress Doll, Barbie Careers Cupcake Chef, Totally Hair 25th Anniversary Barbie Doll, and the Barbie Ice Skater Doll are just some of the popular dolls that inspire girls to dream big!

myself and @gurlstalk. All I hope is that some little girl out there sees this and realizes that her wildest dreams are possible if she puts her mind to it. I hear you and see you, this doll is for you."

With all these amazing choices, what are the most popular Barbie dolls? In March 2018, the *Wall Street Journal* did a survey based on average ratings of the most-reviewed Barbie dolls on Amazon.com. Here's what they found: I Can Be . . . Zookeeper came in first, followed by the Look Doll. In third place was Barbie Fashionistas Silver Stars doll, but fourth place went to Harley-Davidson Ken. The Barbie Look: Lace Dress Doll held fifth place. Cupcake Chef, I Love Valentines, Ice Skater, Totally Hair 25th Anniversary, and Director Nikki rounded out the top ten. These dolls represented different ethnicities, hair styles and textures, and careers, at the same time that they shared being Barbie—or Ken.

The variety and popularity of Barbie's many incarnations don't come close to capturing the imaginative form Barbie takes in the minds of children all over the world. And parents, ever watchful of their daughters' activities, are often drawn into the world of Barbie play.

In the small city of Dawson Creek, on the windy prairie of British Columbia, Canada, Hannah O'Brien was coloring with her daughter in a Barbie coloring book. She noticed that her daughter had made Barbie's eyes an eerie green, and when she asked her daughter about it, she said, "Well, Mom, she is a zombie. Look at her eyes! And she shoots lightning out her hands." As this surprised mother concluded, "I'm not certain that lightning zombie was one of the careers Ruth Handler had envisioned for Barbie, but it proves the point that she really can be anything, and so can any of us."

Anastassia Smorodinskaya, who came to the United States when she was younger from Moscow, Russia, remembers creating complicated stories with her friend around Barbie's various activities. She says, "We'd all sit around discussing each doll's personality, backstory, fears, and dreams." The dolls could be rich or poor, and any age, with all kinds of personalities and problems in their fictional lives.

TOP: Academy Award–winning director Ava DuVernay poses with the Barbie doll made in her likeness in 2015. **BOTTOM**: Ballerina Misty Copeland poses with the doll made in her likeness, complete with vibrant bodysuit and headpiece in 2016.

Breaking Boundaries | 77

One mom showed her daughter a variety of Barbie dolls without saying what they were. She wanted to see her seven-year-old's reaction. Her daughter decided that the President Barbie was a dog-walker, and the Cat Burglar Barbie was a spy. Children's boundless imaginations are what determine Barbie play.

Ruth Handler is the spirit behind the first Entrepreneur Barbie, introduced in 2014. Inspired by Ruth's imagining of the doll in the early 1950s to today, Mattel collaborated with female-founded and -led companies like Girls Who Code, Rent the Runway, and Plum Alley. Their women leaders offer powerful insights about girls having business role models.

Reshma Saujani started and runs the nonprofit Girls Who Code. The group works to support and increase the number of women in computer science. Key to their mission is changing the image of what a computer programmer looks like. (Hint: they don't have to be men.)

Saujani says she works with lots of young girls who play with dolls. And girls need lots of role models to think about who they want to be. She remembers a Barbie when she was young that looked like she was from India, which Saujani loved. Having Barbie dolls of different races lets girls see themselves in the doll. Saujani hopes women will take risks, do something hard, and not be discouraged by

ABOVE: (From left to right) From the Barbie Career Dolls line, shown here are the Barbie Scientist Career Doll with Microscope, Barbie I can Be . . . Ballerina Doll, and Barbie I can Be . . . Mars Explorer Doll.

others telling them they can't do what they want to do, including coding.

At Plum Alley, women entrepreneurs can get funding to start a business through a crowd-funded source. Deborah Jackson, one of the founders, is passionate about women stepping up, owning companies, raising money, becoming successful, and generating their own wealth. She says the Entrepreneur Barbie doll can help not only girls, but also fathers and boys, to see what female entrepreneurs are capable of. She loves that Barbie has a broad range of careers, just as the women she funds have limitless ideas for becoming entrepreneurs.

Rent the Runway is the place to go onlilne for women to rent designer dresses and accessories. How fun does that sound? Jennifer Fleiss is a cofounder of the company. She wants women of all ages to dream bigger and believes that Barbie encourages them to do that from the time they are little girls.

Ruth Handler would be pleased to hear the words of these modern women entrepreneurs who recognize the essential and enduring play value of Barbie. What she envisioned more than sixty years ago still represents so much vision and opportunity to millions of women and girls worldwide.

ABOVE: (From left to right) More Barbie Career Dolls inspired to help little girls dream big, including the Barbie Career of the Year Film Director Doll, the Barbie Careers Game Developer Doll, and the Barbie Entrepreneur Doll. **FOLLOWING**: A collection of Barbie dolls showcasing hundreds of the careers Barbie has taken on throughout the past sixty years.

chapter 4

SHAPING BARBIE

If you wanted to make your own doll, you would be in good company. Humans have made dolls for thousands of years. Early dolls in Egypt and Greece were made of wood or clay and were used in religious ceremonies. From Rome to Japan, doll making was part of early civilization. Cloth and animal bone, corn husks and bark, all served to make representations of humans and grew to be part of children's imaginative play.

But over time, dolls became more sophisticated and elaborate. Artisans in Germany and France made exquisite dolls from porcelain and even more fragile wax. And in America, children cherish dolls from the Old World and also made new ones from wood and clay.

When Ruth Handler first conceived of the Barbie doll, she knew that the detail she wanted could only be made from plastic. But forming dolls from plastic was a completely new method, tried only in Germany. Polystyrene, a form of plastic, was the main raw material for the special injection-molding process that Ruth needed. But she also needed low-cost production, which meant going to Japan, where a recovering post-war economy had kept wages low.

If you like to bake, you have an idea of what was required in the process of making the first Barbie dolls. Baking requires taking separate raw ingredients and forming them into a three-dimensional shape. Think of a loaf, cupcake, or Bundt cake. You need a mold that will give you the shape you have in mind. But if you want a cake that looks like a giraffe, you might not be able to find the right mold. You might need to fashion it yourself using separate molds for different parts. And you need to know just how the various ingredients will react with each other once they are heated in the mold.

OPPOSITE: Designers carefully paint lips and eyes on the dolls by hand.

United States Patent Office

3,425,155
Patented Feb. 4, 1969

Patented Feb. 4, 1969   J. W. RYAN ET AL   **3,425,155**

DOLL CONSTRUCTION FOR NATURAL MOVEMENTS AND POSITIONS

Filed July 15, 1966   Sheet 1 of 2

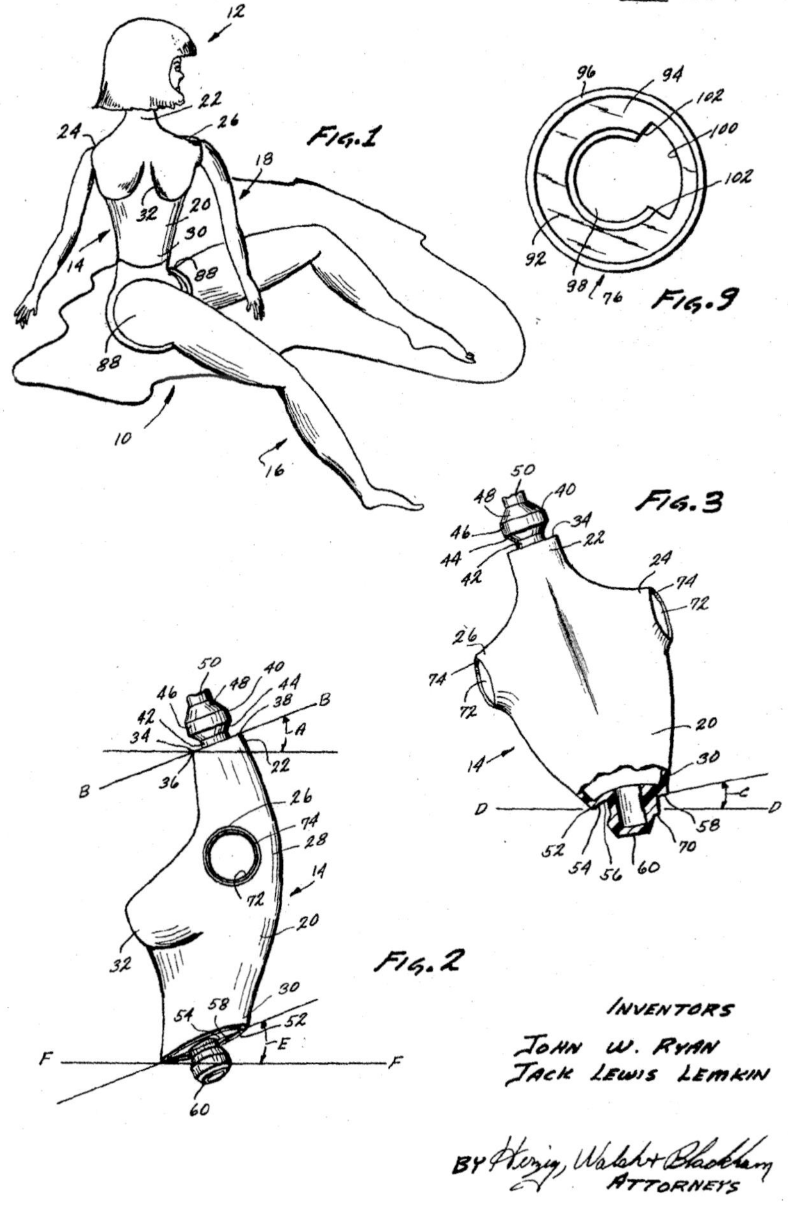

FIG. 1

FIG. 9

FIG. 3

FIG. 2

INVENTORS
JOHN W. RYAN
JACK LEWIS LEMKIN

BY Henzig, Walsh & Blackham
ATTORNEYS

3,425,155
DOLL CONSTRUCTION FOR NATURAL MOVE-
MENTS AND POSITIONS
John W. Ryan, Bel Air, and Jack Lewis Lemkin, Torrance,
Calif., assignors to Mattel, Inc., Hawthorne, Calif., a
corporation of California
Filed July 15, 1966, Ser. No. 565,577
U.S. Cl. 46—162   8 Claims
Int. Cl. A63h 3/36, 3/14, 3/46

ABOVE: Mattel's U.S. Patent for "Doll Construction for Natural Movements and Positions," filed by designer Jack Ryan on June 15, 1966.

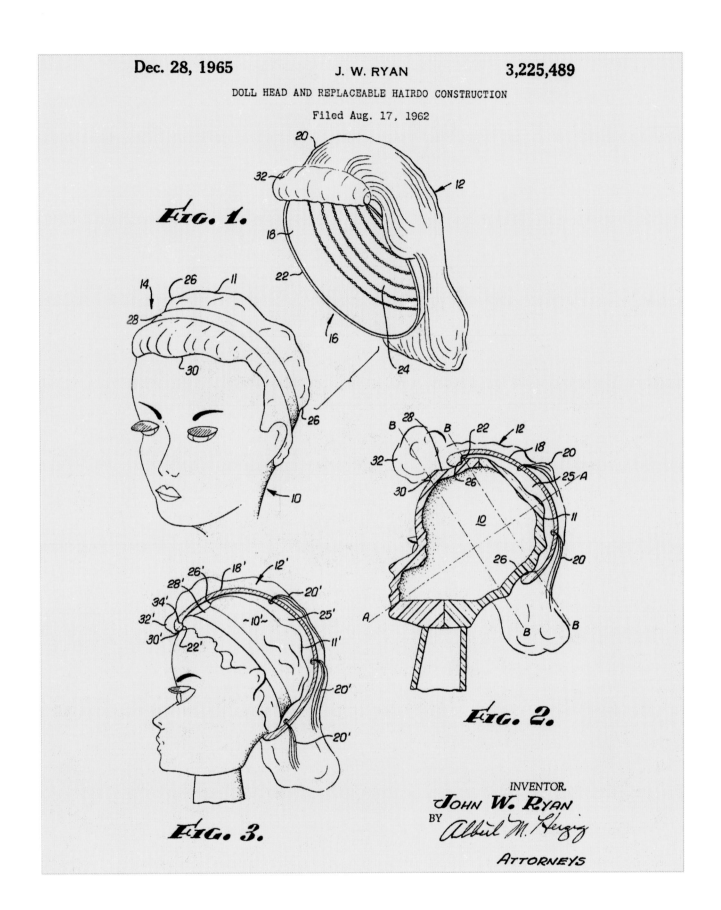

Dec. 28, 1965   J. W. RYAN   3,225,489

DOLL HEAD AND REPLACEABLE HAIRDO CONSTRUCTION

Filed Aug. 17, 1962

Fig. 1.

Fig. 2.

Fig. 3.

INVENTOR.

John W. Ryan

BY *Albert M. Herzig*

ATTORNEYS

ABOVE: Mattel's U.S. Patent for "Doll Head and Replaceable Hairdo Construction," filed by Jack Ryan on August 17, 1962.

Ruth found out that the first polystyrene plastic plant had just been completed near Nagoya, Japan, in 1957, after nearly a year of construction. Japan was ready to make the bowls, cups, glasses, food containers, electrical appliances, and toys that the new world of plastics had ushered in. But no one had "baked" a Barbie doll before, and everything from the raw materials to the molds and the cooking process was an experiment.

Most plastic dolls are made from vinyl. There are other raw materials too, including paint for the face and nails, nylon for the hair, and fabric and accessories for the clothes. But the first step for Ruth was forming Barbie's body.

At the plant in Japan, metal molds were made for Barbie's head, legs, arms, and body. Each mold had multiple cavities so that more than one part could be made at once. The mold cavities were filled with the liquid mixture that became hardened plastic, the way the liquid custard mixture of milk, butter, eggs, and flour becomes a solid cake. Each mold was filled with a measured amount of liquid plastic, and then the mold was closed tight. The molds then went into a heated oven, where they were rotated.

As the mold heated up and turned, the material was pulled by centrifugal force into every crevice, and the inside fused together, became denser, and took the shape

ABOVE: A collection of vintage career dolls. From left to right, the Busy Gal Fashion Barbie (1960), Registered Nurse Barbie (1961), American Airlines Stewardess (1961), and Career Girl Barbie Doll (1963).

of the mold. After the heat was turned off inside the oven, the molds were slowly cooled by air and cold water. After the cooling was complete, the molds were taken from the oven and opened, and the finished pieces were taken out. If needed, trimming was done by hand for any excess plastic that hung off a part. Barbie's finished body part was thrown into a bin, ready for assembly.

But just like Ruth wasn't seen in public without her makeup, Barbie couldn't be assembled until her face was put on. On the first Barbie dolls, each face was painted by hand, using the tiniest brushes. If you look closely at the first dolls, you can see the brush strokes. Soon after, a head-sized mask was made that exposed only those places on Barbie's face to be spray-painted, like using a stencil. This created a much more uniform makeup job for Barbie. Then Barbie's bald head was covered with nylon hair rooted in the vinyl. Special sewing machines, operated by hand, put the hair in place. A comb-out came next, and finally a trim, and then Barbie was ready to have her head put on her shoulders.

After Barbie's bathing suit was slipped on, she was tossed into her narrow box. She was ready to be shipped across the ocean to her first owners. Imagine Ruth's excitement at finally being able to sell the toy creation she had been fighting to make for so long!

Barbie production has moved from Japan to Indonesia and Chang'an, China. In spite of these new developments, the way Barbie is made has not changed. There is still an intense up-front process of design.

As Isela Scaglione, vice president of Product Development for Barbie explains, "We start with what mothers and daughters think about the doll. Millennial audiences wanted something more meaningful and purposeful, and made us rethink how we were marketing the brand. We look back to the past to guide the future, and that's how we're most successful, and right now being a purposeful brand is important.

"Storytelling has shifted from the things Barbie has, to what she does. In the past, there was a focus on a boyfriend or shoes, but now relationships have greater importance,

ABOVE: From left to right, sketches that inspired the fashions for Barbie: Red Flare (1962), After Five (1962), Dinner at Eight (1963), and Orange Blossom (1961).

along with the idea of being anything. What does Barbie enable in a girl?"

From that foundation, designers bring their creativity and imagination to the process. What dolls, clothes, and accessories will match the cultural moment and the brand's narrative for Barbie?

Robert Best, senior design director, says, "You're always looking at culture through sites like Pinterest, or bloggers, or fashion websites and fashion apps. Just like in the old days, there are also still magazine and books. But inspiration can come from going to a museum exhibit like the *Heavenly Bodies* exhibit at the Metropolitan Museum of Art in New York City." Designers take their ideas and build a "mood board," which shows what cultural references are informing their design. Best says, "How do you communicate the idea of culture, what's cool, what's hip, what makes a celebrity the one that's wildly popular? It's like catching lightning in a bottle." Beyond the creative spark, every product in the brand also has to have an analysis of costs and timing required for stores like Walmart and Target. Companies that sell the Barbie brand have different requirements and different dates for when they need products. All these decisions require precise planning. There are two main seasons in the toy cycle. For the spring season, toys must be shipped right after Christmas. For the Christmas season, toys have to be shipped by the first of June.

These deadlines drive the process, and there are many meetings between departments in the Barbie brand to approve the many steps that get a product from idea to market. But as in the beginning, there is still tooling, debugging, production, shipping, and marketing.

As Scaglione explains, "Once we know the design and review samples, we have to build the tools and tool design, then we cut the tools out of blocks of steel and debug them to make sure that the mold is perfect. When we take out the final plastic piece, we want it to be perfect."

Robert Best explains, "We have development partners overseas who are our liaisons on the ground with the factory, and they can use a sketch that we send them as a road map, so that's a jumping-off point for them. If you look at a Fashionista doll, the plant can produce a prototype

ABOVE: A few of the various stages in creating new Barbie doll models, including (from top to bottom) sculpting the head out of clay, creating metal casts for molds, and applying hair and makeup before assembly.

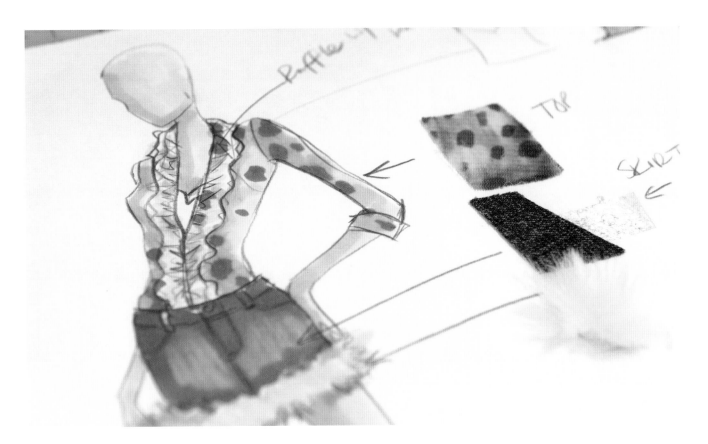

from a general outline. They know the body is going to be one of several. If it's soft goods, meaning fabric, it has to be sewn, and the digital programs can't replicate fabric, so you have to see the real thing. That's why they have to ship a prototype to us, which can take a few days."

The team that designs the dolls is also designing clothes. Doll design involves everything from head to toe, just like fashion. All aspects are in the designers' purview, from clothing to hair and makeup to how the face is sculpted.

The team must also look at the ability to reuse items. They want to minimize waste, so making shoes that can dress a style up or down, for instance, is a consideration. The brand team is always considering how to reuse or repurpose items in the future. And every change has broad implications. For instance, when the flat-footed Barbie was introduced, because of the recognition that women don't always wear high heels, it also meant that none of Barbie's old shoes would fit the new doll. As Best says, "Manufacturing excels in simplicity, because it's more efficient. Variety is the enemy of manufacturing because it's less efficient."

Multiple bodies and shoes also must be tested to see how consumers will react. The brand team is always looking at making exciting new offerings and attracting new fans, even as they consider the complicated process of bringing new items to market.

And just like a cake that slumps on one side, there may be issues with the art on the box, with a fabric's feel, or with parts that don't fit quite right. There may be a need for color adjustment or other tweaks to refine what was approved in the beginning. When new colors are being used, they need special attention.

The 2018 Yves Saint Laurent (YSL) dolls are an example of commitments made with outside partners and how the Barbie team works to fulfill them. Mattel reached out to YSL executives to see if they would be interested in allowing their dresses to be recreated for Barbie. Scaglione explains, "Barbie is a big influence for designers, as well as a product that is influenced by them. We look for partnerships that inspire us, or that we can inspire. So, because of Yves Saint Laurent's standing in the high-fashion industry, we felt it

ABOVE: A rough designer's sketch with mood board, complete with fabric samples. This design would become part of the 2005 Fashion Fever Barbie Animal Print Collection.

ABOVE: A set of Yves Saint Laurent dolls honoring the French fashion designer, which are part of a limited platinum collection of Barbie dolls, released in 2018. There were less than one thousand made of each doll.

would be a win-win to bring that high fashion to a different set of people."

No YSL design had ever been licensed outside the brand before. But YSL agreed, and three dolls, sculpted in the images of the models who first wore the designs, were created to wear the iconic fashions. Only a thousand pieces of each garment were made. Commitments were made by Mattel at every step of the design, including quality, color, and authenticity, right down to how the dresses were constructed. The famous Mondrian dress had each of its geometric solid color patches sewn together separately, just as was done on the original YSL dresses.

Fashion is a form of self-expression and culture, and Barbie parallels that, even down to her face paint. A good example is Malibu Barbie, where the doll looks straight ahead, rather than to the side. Barbie's initial heavily outlined eyes, blue shadow, and red lips were the palette for 1950s women, but when lips turned pale, so did Barbie's.

Barbie's changing face is still sculpted and painted, requiring great artistic talent, as it did in the 1950s.

At Toy Fair in 1959, Ruth was not satisfied with the face of the first Barbie, which was molded by a Japanese sculptor named Kohei Suzuki. It wasn't until Barbie Number Three, released in 1960, that Ruth felt that the arched eyebrows had been smoothed enough to soften her look. Her heavy black eyeliner disappeared as well, giving her a younger appearance. But in the Face Design department at Mattel, changes continued to be made. According to Hiroe Okubo-Worf, one of the early painters, face design was a competition to see which of half a dozen

ABOVE: Two Gold Label Barbie dolls for the adult collector, including the Versace Barbie doll, released in 2004 (left), and the Oscar de la Renta Barbie doll, released in 2016 (right).

painters could do the best job. Okubo-Worf's talent stood out, and for many years she was the sole face painter for Barbie. She saw many changes, including 1967's Twist 'n Turn with deep red lips, rosy cheekbones, and large blue eyes with long lashes. Malibu Barbie recieved a smile showing her teeth in 1971. In 1979, Kissing Barbie was sold with a pucker on her lips that could be relaxed through a button on the back. The introduction of the international dolls series in 1980 meant further changes in face sculpting and painting.

In the ensuing years, there have been Barbies sculpted to look like actual people, including celebrities and notables from the Shero and Inspiring Women lines, that mirror the looks of the extraordinary women they are celebrating through face shape, paint, hair, and body. Equally challenging for the artists are the Fashionista dolls, each one a Barbie with a unique face. There are more than forty Fashionista dolls, with more being created all the time by Mattel artists. Once a sculpt is approved, it goes to the plant, where they might do a rapid prototype using three-dimensional printing, a process almost unimaginable in the 1950s! From there, designers can consider the design, make changes, and move to the approvals that will get Barbie to market.

Perhaps the most dramatic sculpting change for Barbie came in 2016, when her single iconic body type was expanded. Kimberly Culmone, vice president and global head of Barbie Design, tells the inside story of Barbie's new bodies.

Kim Culmone isn't sure when she got her first Barbie, but it was before she turned four years old, and the love affair is still going. Kim explains, "Barbie played a gigantic role in my life. I had yellow and orange versions of the Dreamhouse. I had the pool and the Corvette. I also had lots of Legos and a pellet rifle, but Barbie was always my top number-one item. I keep my favorite Barbie from my childhood in my office. It's Beauty Secrets Barbie, which had a feature where her arms could be moved by a button, but I liked the things she came with, like powder puffs and toothbrushes and her super-long blonde hair. I adored her, and she got to go on vacation with me."

ABOVE: The Kissing Barbie doll, released in 1979, was dressed in a sheer pale pink nylon dress with a floral and kiss imprint pattern with a tiny pink nylon ribbon accent, and pink superstar shoes. The Kissing Barbie came with a bouquet of pink and purple plastic flowers, and play lipstick for Barbie.

Kim grew up in New Orleans, an only child and an only grandchild on her Dad's side, so she had lots of people buying her Barbie dolls. Even in high school she received them as gifts, and she remembers getting a Holiday Barbie in college. Her twenty-fifth birthday party was built around a Barbie theme. She seemed destined to have Barbie play a bigger role in her life.

Kim was the first in her family to go to college. She earned a degree in interior design and then a second degree in fabric design. She opened a textile design studio, working for big apparel companies doing print work, weaving, and knitting. She created designs that were then sent overseas to be made. But she decided to build her résumé with an in-house job and found a temporary assignment at Mattel in Textile Engineering. That was the department that developed fabrics for all Mattel toys, including Barbie.

"All of a sudden," Kim recalls, "my mind was blown. I hadn't really thought about the idea that someone had to design Barbie! There were all these fantastic artists that were doing painting, textiles, hair, fashion. I

ABOVE: Shown from left to right are the first Hispanic Barbie and the first Black Barbie, both released in 1980.

realized I could take my love as a kid and my textile background and put them together." Kim's eureka moment was the first step in building a career that has changed her—and the doll she loves.

Kim was in awe of the people who worked in the specialties, the talented craftspeople who were part of Barbie's creation. She spent a lot of time watching and learning and looking for the job she wanted, which was to be on Barbie's design team. When an opening came up, Kim was hired into a permanent position designing for Barbie. Years later, in 2013, she was asked to head up all of design for the Barbie brand around the world!

From the beginning, Kim felt keenly responsible for the brand. She explains, "You can't have a founder like Ruth Handler and not be a boundary pusher. We call on her in our spirit. On an emotional sense and as brand guardian, I

want to protect the brand because of Ruth, because we influence so many people with what we create."

But soon after Kim took on her new position, Barbie sales slowed. Everyone agreed that a revolution was needed, and top leadership was saying they were open to ideas they hadn't been open to before. "That's a designer's dream," according to Kim.

Changing Barbie's body has been a topic for a long time. It was obvious from the marketplace that there was a desire to explore new body types. But the idea hadn't always tested well in terms of consumer demand.

Kim and her team were listening to consumers intently and realized their vision for Barbie wasn't getting through, so they took a hard look at themselves. Kim says, "I went to my family of designers and asked, 'What have you always wanted to do that you've never done before? If you

ABOVE: In 2016, Mattel added three new body types to its Barbie Fashionistas line, including (from left to right) petite, tall, and curvy, alongside the original figure, to offer girls choices that are more reflective of their worlds. The collection of thirty-three new dolls includes twenty-four hair styles, fourteen different face sculpts, and seven skin tones.

were Ruth Handler today, how would you want to live up to our promise of being reflective of the times, and being inspiring of limitless potential for children?'" She wanted them to dream big. "I wanted people to show up as their authentic selves and create a collective tapestry of taste and experience to get our creations to their highest expression."

The team responded with a range of ideas that have all been implemented and are continuing to be built on. But it wasn't easy to make such a revolutionary change. There were dissenters who felt Barbie might lose her appeal. Kim says, "My role is to keep Barbie on the cutting edge, and that can make things uncomfortable. But that's our role in creative, to make the unseen seen. I like the saying 'The best way to predict the future is to create it.' I have to place bets." She and her team bet on changes that reflected diversity and inclusion, and the bet paid off.

ABOVE: In 2017, Mattel expanded its Ken Fashionistas line with fifteen new Ken dolls, featuring three body types. Shown here from left to right are the broad, original, and slim. The new line also features seven skin tones, eight hair colors, and nine hair styles.

ABOVE: In 1997, Mattel announced a special edition Barbie friend named "Share-a-Smile Becky," who used a pink and purple wheelchair, and who comes with two friendship necklaces to give to other friends.

Barbie's traditional blue eyes and blonde hair grew to a more inclusive reflection of society. Barbie's perpetual high heel also became a flexible version that could be a flat or high heel–shaped foot, as well as a permanently flat version. While Barbie had long reflected other ethnicities through skin tone, the team began to change the sculpts for her face to reflect ethnic characteristics. And, perhaps most dramatically, Barbie's famous figure, long legged and voluptuous, became just one of four body types: original, curvy, petite, and tall.

Diversity and inclusion rose to the top of concerns for designers and marketing. And once they had opened the door to questioning Barbie's presentation, they suddenly saw things they had not seen before, like the way Barbie was presented in illustrations and on media platforms. Kim says, "The culture is also showing more diversity and inclusion, and we're watching and being responsive."

The body diversity dolls are going into the Fantasy and Career line, and Ken received new body types too. Even specialty and collector dolls have body diversity. And the best-selling doll in 2017 was a curvy Fashionista. Kim's department is committed to continuing to think of ways to support the values of diversity and inclusion held by the brand. A line of differently abled dolls, one in a wheelchair and one with a prosthetic leg, will be introduced in 2019. Kim says, "We want people to see themselves reflected in the brand."

Could the new body types have been even more diverse? Kim explains that the Barbie brand is a "system of play." "We looked at all possibilities for the body. But variety complicates the system. We wanted bodies where we could have some sort of universal fit. We want them to share clothes as much as possible, so we made bodies that work for that idea."

How hard was it to make this enormous change in an iconic global brand? Kim says, "I often told my team on the bad days that they should think about Ruth Handler. I stand on her shoulders, and the shoulders of so many other women who came before me, and I'm really proud to lead this charge, and hopefully leaving the brand better than I found it, better for the world and the next

generation of leaders on Barbie. It feels like a calling more than a job."

Kim is convinced that Barbie is forever. She feels that Ruth Handler created the doll with a clear human truth at her core that will endure: that a girl can be anything she wants to be. She believes that the brand must stay on the cutting edge, like Jill Barad, the former CEO, did when she brought out the Shani collection, the first line of African American fashion dolls—and like she is doing with dolls reflecting diversity and inclusion.

Kim says, "Barbie is, and always has been, a revolutionary brand. We have to be reflective of the consumers who are shopping for her today, and then there's no stopping Barbie."

ABOVE: One of Mattel's newest career dolls is the Barbie 60th Anniversary Pilot Doll, released in 2019, dressed in a blue pilot's uniform with a matching pilot's cap and black boots. **FOLLOWING**: In 2016, Mattel introduced Barbie dolls with diverse body types with new shapes and sizes for Barbie and friends, including petite, tall, thin, and curvy.

chapter 5

BARBIE LIFESTYLE

Barbie's first fans were quick to let Mattel know that they wanted Barbie to have a friend. There were thousands of letters asking specifically for a boyfriend for Barbie. This made perfect sense to Ruth. She had seen her own daughter playing with both female and male paper dolls.

The late 1950s and early 1960s were a time marked by high expectations for home and family. On television, families watched *Father Knows Best*, *The Adventures of Ozzie and Harriet,* and *Dennis the Menace,* all showing traditional families of the time. The women on these shows, up to any challenge, had equally great husbands. Surely, children would buy a male doll to go with Barbie.

But once again, toy buyers did not embrace the idea of a male doll. Boy dolls did not have a good sales history, and the buyers didn't believe that Barbie's success would transfer to an adult male doll.

In characteristic fashion, Ruth moved ahead despite the doubters. But she almost stumbled on an obvious hurdle. It was one thing to give Barbie breasts, but should Ken be anatomically correct? She thought there should be a suggestion of male anatomy, a bulge, however slight. Charlotte Johnson, who would expand her clothes designs to the new doll, agreed with Ruth. But the male design team pushed back, wanting no hint of genitalia at all.

Ruth accused them of having no guts.

Prototypes were ordered with varying degrees of a bulge that would show in underwear. In the end, the doll's crotch area was as flat as his stomach and looked as unrealistic as Ruth and Charlotte had feared when the very first red bathing trunks were in place. But Ruth gave in to the research-and-design team's concerns that a doll that was anything less than neutered would hurt Mattel.

Ken debuted on March 11, 1961, at Toy Fair. He had the

OPPOSITE: Ruth Handler with a collection of Barbie and Ken dolls from the early 1960s.

ABOVE LEFT: The original Bathing Suit Barbie and Ken from 1959. TOP RIGHT: From an early 1960s Mattel advertisement showing a young girl smiling at a collection with Barbie, Ken, and their friends. BOTTOM RIGHT: A 1963 advertisement for Barbie and Ken's Hot Rod and Sports Car, built to fit the Barbie, Ken, and Midge dolls.

barest hint of a smile, better for children to imagine his personality and moods. He came with blond or brunette hair that was made of felt, but it rubbed off easily, especially when wet, and was soon replaced with plastic hair molded to his head. He wouldn't get rooted hair like Barbie until 1973. Sandals with a red strap matched his red trunks, and he carried a yellow terry cloth towel. Like Barbie, he was ready for the many outfits to come.

Ken, named for Ruth's son, was introduced in the Mattel catalog with the tag line "He's a doll!" Barbie was a "Teen-age Fashion Model," but Ken's description was "Barbie's Boyfriend." He was 12 inches tall, and his television debut came in a commercial where he appears to be in a ballroom. The commercial tells a story of Barbie and Ken's relationship starting "at the dance," where Barbie "knew that she and Ken would be going together." Their coordinated outfits could be used for outings at the beach or fraternity dances or even a wedding. Barbie's Wedding Day Set included a blue garter, and Ken's Tuxedo had a white boutonniere. As with Charlotte Johnson's Barbie clothes, Ken's outfits had all the precision, quality, and detail that buyers had come to expect.

According to her growing number of fans, Barbie needed a female friend too, and in 1963, freckle-faced Midge Hadley went on sale. Midge was Barbie's best friend and would later marry Allan, introduced in 1964. That same year, Barbie got a younger teenage sister named Skipper. Barbie's family really grew the next year when the preschool-age twins, Tutti and Todd, were introduced. And in 1966 Barbie got a cousin named Francie.

By 1968, Barbie had her first African American friend, Christie. She was part of a talking dolls group, each programmed to say short phrases that varied by doll. In a nod to the British Invasion, Stacey, a friend of Barbie's from the United Kingdom, also arrived in 1968. In her talking version, she had a British accent, and she was only made for three years. Her face sculpt would later be used for Malibu Barbie. And in recognition of the hippie era, hip and mod PJ was introduced in 1969, with beaded ties on her pigtails.

The 1960s also saw the first celebrity Barbie.

ABOVE: Talking Christie, the first African American Barbie doll, was introduced in 1968. The Christie doll shown here is from 1970, and wears a yellow-and-orange print top with orange vinyl trim and orange vinyl shorts.

ABOVE: Twiggy was a cultural icon and prominent teenage model in the 1960s, and Mattel released the Twiggy doll at the height of her career. Shown here is an advertisement from Mattel's 1968 catalog.

Supermodel Twiggy went on sale in 1967 in a vertical-striped minidress and yellow boots. She was advertised as "London's top teen model."

Barbie's family didn't grow again until 1989, when her cousin Jazzie was introduced. Then in 1992, Mattel introduced Barbie's sister Stacie (not to be confused with her British friend Stacey from 1968). In 1995, Kelly (called Shelly in Europe) entered the scene. Kelly went out of production, and Chelsea took her place in 2011 as Barbie's youngest sister at around five or six years old.

Over the decades, Barbie's world has grown exponentially, but the thread that binds the dolls together is their relationships. Some relationships are part of the doll, like Barbie's family and designated friends, and some are relationships built through the potential play value of the various dolls.

Creating dolls that expand Barbie's world and girls' imaginations starts with a team from the Marketing, Design, and Public Relations departments. They brainstorm together about dolls that will be topical, like the recent Barbie Robotics Engineer, and Game Developer dolls. They consider whether the doll will have global resonance, the age at which girls will understand the doll's given role, whether the doll will serve a purpose, and whether it's a doll that can have great play value. For instance, the Robotics Engineer comes with a purple laptop and a tiny silver robot just begging to be "activated." Robert Best, senior design director at Mattel, explains, "We're taking the path of Ruth's promise. We know that girls have a dream gap. Girls don't see themselves in society in as full a way as they can. So it's even more important for us to push that conversation. Yes, Barbie is a fashion doll, but Ruth Handler fought to get this doll out into the world. We have to reflect her fight. It's critical to raise women up and support that with the brand, because we have such a big megaphone."

While children play out stories they know, and core play patterns—like brushing Barbie's hair, dressing the dolls up, nurturing, or playing in the house or yard—are still popular, Mattel has introduced dolls that stretch children's imaginations.

In 2019, the career line introduced a partnership with National Geographic. Along with the Beekeeper Barbie and Butterfly Scientist were dolls that expanded on the idea of being a naturalist. There's a biologist, a conservationist, a photojournalist, and an astrophysicist, all with intriguing accessories. As Robert Best explains, "We give girls what they want, but we also help them stretch their dreams. We pick jobs that girls will relate to."

Key to the Barbie message is showing careers where women are underrepresented. They call the concept "See It/Be It," and girls and their parents love the dolls. All the career dolls fit seamlessly into the world of Barbie, her friends, and her family. They add to the richness of the play universe where Barbie can encounter a new friend at the zoo as easily as at school. Barbie has become a "system of play,"

ABOVE: A vintage Twiggy doll, dressed in the "Turnouts" outfit from 1967, which consisted of a minidress with a striped multicolor bodice and silvertone skirt, accented with a wide silver belt at the hip, and silver boots.

where all her dimensions fit together. A mermaid might be found in Barbie's convertible, or a princess in a doctor's coat and stethoscope. And Barbie embraces difference.

Storytelling packs with accessories allow all the dolls to have adventures, like packs for going to the movies, traveling, being a student, or having a day at the beach.

Barbie's Dreamhouse and accessories have also evolved to accommodate her growing circle of friends and family. The Barbie Dreamhouse used to be designed just for her, but now it has expanded rooms, beds, and even bunkbeds and invites a constellation of dolls for play. Barbie cars and campers have also grown so that inclusion of more characters in play is naturally encouraged. Barbie's family is about relationships and connection. Her three sisters are important to her. Chelsea, the youngest, needs support, but also has a budding personality. Skipper, a young teen, and Stacey, barely an adolescent, offer a full range of play. Nurturing is a popular play pattern, so Skipper is a babysitter. With her own babysitting business, she also encourages the idea of female entrepreneurship.

Barbie also has friends outside of the day-to-day world. Her Dreamtopia line includes mermaids, fairies, and princesses, plus MerBears and Unicorns. These fantasy archetypes have light and sound, but they also have different body types. In Barbie's world, even fantastical play incorporates inclusion and diversity. Fairies with gossamer wings and mermaids with rainbow tails still reflect the wide range of children who play with them.

These play patterns are reinforced by Barbie's television shows. *Barbie's Dreamhouse Adventures,* which started in 2018, is the latest addition to the shows that bring the dolls to life through cartoons. While the previous show, *Barbie Life in the Dreamhouse,* focused on reality show–style crises mostly between a group of Barbie's friends, *Dreamhouse Adventures* is about relationships between Barbie, her family, and a few friends, including Ken. In *Dreamhouse Adventures,* Barbie's mother is a brilliant computer scientist, and Barbie and her sisters are proactive, most often taking the lead in solving problems, and believe they can be anything. *Dreamhouse Adventures* is new, more empowered content because Barbie is sending a message: girls can be anything.

ABOVE: Barbie's space career began in 1965 when Mattel released Miss Astronaut Barbie and Mr. Astronaut Ken doll. Shown here is the 1986 Astronaut Barbie doll, in fashion with the time, dressed in a fuchsia and silver metallic bodysuit top and matchng fuchsia pants with a silver belt and pink over-the-knee boots.

ABOVE: The Barbie lifestyle expanded in various directions, but in 1966 surfing was still all the rage, and Barbie and friends were part of it. Shown here is a Mattel advertisement from 1966 for "The Active World of Barbie," with Barbie, Ken, and Skipper riding the wave. FOLLOWING: Ruth and Elliot Handler with their Barbie and friends lifestyle display at the Canada Toy Show in 1971.

chapter 6

FASHION AND ART

Barbie was destined from the start to have a beautiful wardrobe. She was the brainchild of Ruth Handler, and Ruth loved fashion. Every photo of Ruth from the 1950s shows her in stylish clothes that show off her figure. She was often seen in plaid or bright prints, in a suit with a peplum waist, or in a smart knit. She was shapely and busty, if not long-legged like her creation. But like Barbie, Ruth's hair was cut in the latest fashion, her makeup was perfect, her nails were manicured, and she knew how to accessorize.

In her first Barbie clothing designer, Ruth found a woman like herself. Charlotte Johnson also loved style and fashion. They first met at a coffee shop, probably off Sunset Boulevard, not far from Charlotte's apartment. Soon Charlotte's kitchen table would be her workspace. Her intention from the moment she and Ruth first agreed to work together was to understand both the timelessness

of fashion and the trends that influence change. Charlotte's ideas for Barbie's first outfits grew from Ruth's desire to give girls certain play possibilities.

There were twenty-two outfits in Barbie's first collection, including a satin bridal gown with tulle, a jacket with matching sheath skirts reminiscent of Chanel, the red-and-white stripes of a travel ensemble with a dark blue pencil skirt called Roman Holiday, the fur stole and long white gloves of bubble-skirted Parisienne, and underclothes that girls might not yet be using, but could anticipate, including a bra and a slip, baby doll pajamas, and a full-length negligee and peignoir.

With their party dresses, school sportswear, swimsuits, and an ensemble perfect for an afternoon at the movies, outfits like Resort Set, Suburban Shopper, and Saturday Matinee were suggestive of activities that appealed to girls.

OPPOSITE: Artist and fashion designer BillyBoy* posing with one of his dolls. He had a collection of more than eleven thousand Barbie dolls and three thousand Ken dolls. He also authored the 1987 book *Barbie: Her Life and Time*s. From 1984–90, Mattel sponsored two fashion tours curated by BillyBoy*, and later he worked as both a designer and consultant for Mattel, where he designed two Barbie dolls.

Ruth wanted a ballet outfit, so Barbie got lace-up ballet shoes, a crown, and a program indicating she was dancing in *The Nutcracker* as the Sugar Plum Fairy. Ruth also wanted to be sure there were outfits for more ordinary activities, like going to prom, a football game, or a job. She thought girls would have more interest in Barbie if she were more like them and less glamorous. But over time, it became clear that girls liked glamour as well.

Charlotte also shared Ruth's absolute focus on quality. She was driven and detail oriented. Within Mattel, Ruth was known for her relentless quality control. She would shut down a product line for a month if she had to, losing tens of thousands of dollars, to make sure that a toy met her specifications. She expected the same from Barbie's clothes, and Charlotte delivered.

Charlotte and Ruth agreed that Charlotte needed to go to Japan to oversee clothing production for Barbie. She traveled to Japan on one of the early jet flights, accompanied by some of the male Mattel executives, including Elliot Handler, but once in Japan, the men went off to work on dollhouse furniture.

Charlotte was introduced to Fumiko Miyatsuka, who would be her assistant. Fumiko had never met an American woman, and she spoke no English. Charlotte spoke no Japanese, but the two managed—through hand signals, facial expressions, and a shared love of fashion—to work together for a year. Together they would scour Tokyo to find fabrics and prints that would fit the tiny mannequin they were charged with dressing.

Tokyo, still scarred by bombing from World War II, had embraced American culture. Ninety-nine percent of Japanese television shows were American, including *Superman*, though it included a Japanese voice-over. Sony had just come out with all-transistor portable televisions, making American influence even more widespread. Golf became enormously popular, and girls swung Hula-

---

ABOVE: A Barbie lookalike poses next to the new Barbie U.S. postage stamp in El Segundo, California, on August 24, 1999. As Barbie celebrated her 40th anniversary, the stamp was one of the winners in a public vote in a series celebrating the 20th century.

ABOVE: Mbili Barbie, released in 2002, as part of Mattel's innovative Treasures of Africa Collection created by New York designer Byron Lars. She is dressed in a ribbed corset of multi-colored beads accenting her intricately woven, backless sweater; a skirt featuring a ruffled waist and shirred V-line design, a full bustle is composed of ostrich feathers, and Azure blue boots.

Hoops, just as their American counterparts did during the 1958 craze.

But the Japanese interest in America couldn't change the fact that Charlotte found herself in a world where everything from food to language was worlds apart from anything she had known. When having dinner at the Imperial Hotel, where she lived, she would reach out to any American who might come through. She must have been lonely, hungry to hear her native tongue and to have some feeling of contact with the home she left so far behind. But her main anchor—and her salvation—came through her work. She would soon turn real fashion into doll fashion.

One night a beautiful man and woman came into the hotel dining room. The woman had on a bubble dress, first made by Balenciaga. It's possible that seeing that dress in person inspired Charlotte's design for Barbie's Gay Parisienne dress.

TOP: Famous French hairdresser Louis Alexandre Raimon, known as Alexandre de Paris, styles Barbie's hair in Paris on November 25, 1993. **BOTTOM**: Bloomingdales and Mattel present one-of-a-kind *Hairspray* Ken and Barbie dolls, with Ken as Edna Turnblad and Barbie as Tracy Turnblad.

ABOVE: Jewelry designer Tarina Tarantino arrives at "The Pink Plastic Party of the Year" to celebrate the launch of the Tarina Tarantino Barbie doll and jewelry collection, at the Tarina Tarantino Boutique on July 17, 2008 in Los Angeles, California.

Charlotte started by using the "TPO" method of design. *T* for the time of day when a fashion piece would be worn, *P* for the place Barbie would wear the clothing, and *O* for the occasion where the fashion would be worn.

Although lingerie was designed for Barbie in the initial line, Charlotte decided that there was little play value in underwear, and that a bathing suit would offer more play opportunity and spark imagination as soon as the package was opened. That's why tens of thousands of Barbie dolls would first be seen dressed for a dip in the pool or ocean.

Charlotte's initial inspiration for Barbie's clothes came from *Vogue* magazine, as well as *Vogue* sewing patterns, where the pictures on the covers gave her ideas. She had

to think of everything, like creating a stuffed dog to go with Barbie's negligee and the pink plastic hand mirror with Barbie's logo on the back. But Charlotte would be known simply as "CJ" on the boxes that held her creations.

Charlotte also incorporated her knowledge of production and her understanding of how clothes could be constructed. She was on the lookout for simplicity in sewing design. For instance, the bathing suit was composed of only two darts and one seam. Barbie's clothes were die cut, so Charlotte could be sure of the precision of the cuts. Bradley Justice, an expert on Charlotte Johnson, has taken apart every outfit from 1959 to understand how they were made. He says, "There was magic in Charlotte's pattern-making and skill."

ABOVE: Actress Angela Griffin (left) and Angela Rippon (right), Chairman of English National Ballet, pose in 2001 with a Barbie doll in London, when it was announced that the National Ballet had signed a sponsorship deal with Mattel to stage Tchaikovsky's *The Nutcracker*.

Barbie was also given a twinset, a knitted sweater vest with a matching long-sleeve sweater over it. Twinsets were very popular in the 1950s. Charlotte found a Japanese knitting factory to make the sweaters. The first order was for two hundred and fifty thousand, before Ruth knew whether Barbie would even sell! But the twinset turned out to be very popular and was reordered.

Charlotte and Fumiko were always on the hunt for the right fabrics and materials, including the many flowers that were used. Barbie's original silk flowers came from a legendary Japanese silk flower maker, Hiroshi Fukushima. For all the tiny zippers, Charlotte found YKK, a zipper manufacturer. It was the first time they had made zippers that were size 0. The fun of using those miniature zippers led to many letters from little girls wanting more!

The Tokyo fabric district was a favorite haunt of Charlotte and Fumiko. But they couldn't always find what they wanted. One time Charlotte bought a woman's slip at a department store and ripped off the lace in order to get just what she wanted for Barbie. Fumiko was horrified at the waste of the garment, but Charlotte, like Ruth, wasn't going to let anything stand in the way of a perfect wardrobe for Barbie.

Charlotte would send Fumiko to the factories with very precise specifications for the clothes, and woe be to the manufacturer who tried to make even the slightest change. Charlotte's painstaking preparation needed to be respected.

Inspiration could come from anywhere, even a rice bowl. Barbie's Suburban Shopper hat was modeled on a rice bowl cover that Charlotte had once seen. Similarly, Fumiko was washing up when she discovered that the bottom of the spigot was the same size as Barbie's head. Fumiko, after warning Charlotte not to turn on the water, formed the hat for the Picnic Set around the faucet, and a new hat was born.

At the end of Charlotte's time in Japan, she and Fumiko had made twenty-two new designs. These designs were modern and cutting edge, and still maintained a 1950s flavor, while also anticipating the 1960s. Some people think the first Barbie clothes were inspired by Jackie Kennedy, but

LEFT: Japanese Ballerina Erena Takahashi, 23, the youngest principal dancer of the English National Ballet, in London, dressed as the new Barbie doll at the announcement that the Ballet had signed a sponsorship deal with Mattel to stage *The Nutcracker* by Tchaikovsky. RIGHT: Mattel's Nutcracker Barbie, released in 2001.

ABOVE: Posing on the stairs by her Beverly Hills home, actress and model Corazon Ugalde Yellen Armenta wears an outfit identical to her collector's Barbie doll—an outfit called "Matinee Fashion" from 1965. Armenta had her attire specially made for wearing to Barbie doll convention fashion shows.

ABOVE: This image shows custom Barbie Jewelry designed for a 2003 collection to be sold by auction to benefit the French Red Cross, on December 11, 2003, in Paris, France. This Mikimoto Barbie is dressed in clothes designed by Nina Ricci, including pink crepe silk dress. Barbie is wearing ear pendants, a necklace, and a navel piece made of yellow gold with cultured pearls, and the bracelet is a string of Mikimoto cultured pearls.

she was not yet well known. As Bradley Justice says, "Maybe Jackie copied Barbie."

Back at Mattel, Ruth told Charlotte she would have to go back and forth to Japan to supervise production. She had to hire new designers, so three women who had strong design backgrounds joined Charlotte's team. They would go to International Silk and Wool, still the place Mattel designers go to find material for fashions. Their work would be eagerly awaited by children, especially as Christmas approached. Children would get the Sears Christmas Wish Book, with the word *Toys* in large letters on its cover. Inside were pictures and information on what new Barbie items would be available, including the fashion design team's newest items.

In 1968, a German television documentary crew came to Mattel. Inside the closely guarded confines of the design studio, Charlotte, then fifty years old, wore a Gucci print dress and was surrounded by European fashion magazines. She was recognized as Barbie's "wardrobe mistress." Mattel had become the largest manufacturer of women's apparel, thanks to Ruth's inspiration and Charlotte's creative drive.

ABOVE: The Gianmaria Buccellati Barbie is wearing fashion designed by Michael Kors, including a gray cashmere jersey dress with a gray and anthracite chinchilla stole. Barbie's jewelry, designed by Buccellati, is dual-gold engraved "Primavera" necklace, earrings, and bracelet, encrusted with diamonds and rubies. The Barbie Jewelry 2003 Collection was auctioned on December 11, 2003, in Paris, France, to benefit the French Red Cross.

After twenty years at the top of fashion design for Mattel, Charlotte was honored with a gilded Barbie doll. She had not only dressed Barbie, but also her friends, family, and special dolls like Miss America. "We make miniature fashions, not doll clothes," Charlotte told a reporter. At the award ceremony, Ruth said, "Many could have done what Charlotte did, but no one could have done it better."

Charlotte would be pleased to know that her work not only became collectible, it inspired countless designers and seamstresses like her.

Abby Glassenberg writes a column for *Sew News* magazine called "The Common Thread." She talks about how sewing affects our whole lives and becomes part of our lives. She says, "As an adult who writes about sewing and is involved in the sewing community every day, I noticed that it seemed most people started sewing because they sewed for Barbie. Barbie was like

ABOVE: Paris Hilton attends the Jeremy Scott & Moschino Party with Barbie on December 4, 2014, in Miami Beach, Florida.

a mannequin, a miniature woman, so with a paper towel you could drape a gown and make Barbie haute couture, because she had breasts and hips and long legs, like a fashion model."

Abby knew that patterns that were sold in the 1940s came with miniature mannequins. Children could drape the cloth over these dolls as they worked with the patterns that came from *McCall's* and *Simplicity*. Barbie serves the same purpose for budding sewists.

On the television show *Project Runway*, many contestants talk about having a Barbie and taking scraps of old clothing or rags to start designing. "Barbie really plays a role as a muse for sewing," Abby says. "She's so accessible, and so small and easy to hold, so even with a small amount of fabric or even Kleenex, or a necktie, you can make her a hat or a dress. She's like a canvas that gives you permission to design for her."

Major designers remember starting with Barbie as well. Anna Sui remembers, "I started dressing Barbie dolls with my own designs at an early age." Cynthia Rowley says, "As a little girl, I spent countless hours playing with my Barbie

TOP: Mattel featured an extended line of Barbie figures emphasizing themes of haute couture, Hollywood, and celebrity—including this Marilyn Monroe Giftset Barbie—at the International Toy Fair February in New York on February 10, 2002. BOTTOM: Fashion Bloggers Cailli Beckermann (left) and Sam Beckermann (right), who is wearing a Moschino Barbie sweater, during Art Basel in Miami Beach on December 6, 2014.

dolls, even designing and sewing one-of-a-kind outfits for the doll. I guess you could say Barbie gave me my start as a designer." Jason Wu, who designs for many celebrities, including former First Lady Michelle Obama, first realized his love of fashion designing for Barbie dolls. He loved the dolls, buying them to take apart so he could put them together with makeovers. He's had more than a hundred Barbies that he has used for styling hair. These designers, and more, have created fashions for the Barbie market. Jeremy Scott, who is forty, has given the world eye-popping designs for many pop stars, including Britney Spears, Miley Cyrus, and Katy Perry. He loves to use kitsch and recognizable accessories like cell phones and cell cases, lots of bling, and fun trinkets. As director of the Italian fashion house Moschino, he's revived the brand and started creating for Barbie. His limited-edition Moschino Barbie, with a bright and prominent display of gold bling, was the subject of a first-ever ad for Barbie that featured a little boy. In the ad, the boy, with hair styled like Jermey's, calls the doll "so fierce."

Jeremy told the *New Yorker* he was thrilled. "It's not a fashion story—it's a news story . . . I've done something that's affecting culture." Jeremy is keenly aware of the enormous scope of Barbie's effect on culture. "The thing I love most about Barbie is that she is the ultimate muse. She's worn every style and design imaginable and at the same time she's had every possible profession you can dream of."

Barbie's effect on design and fashion has both drawn from culture and affected it for sixty years. Barbie was born at the end of the 1950s, a decade of rebuilding and recovery in America.

After the trauma of World War II, American soldiers returned from battle looking for stability in work and family life. Women moved from jobs outside the home back to childcare and homemaking roles. In a relieved country looking for order and peace, new ways to play and find enjoyment were born.

Disneyland opened its Magic Kingdom, a land always clean, orderly and full of fun and surprises. Elvis electrified the country with rock 'n' roll music, defining *pop* with

TOP: Dominican American fashion designer Oscar de la Renta (center) poses with models in fashions designed for Mattel's Barbie dolls, at a Barbie Fashion Show in 1984.
BOTTOM: Television host Hofit Golan poses at the Jeremy Scott & Moschino Party with Barbie in Miami Beach, Florida, on December 4, 2014.

both a sensual voice and moves to match. Girls went wild. Parents worried what effect he was having on their daughters, who still wore shirtwaists and pedal pushers and were told to be modest.

Barbie seemed to bridge the divide. She was as revolutionary as Elvis, with her grown-up body, but her clothes reflected the conservative style of the time. Her

Barbie-Q outfit was a prim sundress with a full apron. Her Sweater Girl outfit fully covered her in a turtleneck, vest, and matching sweater and below-the-knee wraparound skirt. And her Wedding Day set was a church wedding gown with formal train, with a mock pearl tiara to hold the long bridal veil.

But Barbie's first outfits quickly changed as the upheavals

ABOVE: A collection of Limited Edition Barbie dolls, dressed in stunning fashions from two of the world's premiere designers. From left to right are the Christian Dior Barbie Doll, released in 1997; the Bob Mackie Gold Barbie doll, released in 1990; and the Christian Dior Barbie Doll, released in 1995.

ABOVE: The Stephen Burrows Pazette Barbie Doll was designed by Linda Kyaw and released in 2012 as part of Mattel's Gold Label line of Barbie dolls. The show-stopping doll was dressed in an extraordinary ensemble, including silvery glitter, rhinestones, and sequins. Her silver-colored headpiece features a cascade of white feathers.

of the 1960s sent every part of America racing toward change. Elvis went in the Army, and a new group called the Beatles showed up on *The Ed Sullivan Show*. Andy Warhol stunned the art world with his paintings of iconic objects like Campbell's soup cans and Coke bottles and celebrities like Marilyn Monroe.

Sean Connery popularized the swoon-inducing character James Bond as movies started to move away from classic cinema and show more sex and violence.

Folk music had a revival. Bob Dylan released the song "The Times They Are a-Changin'" as the civil rights, women's rights, and anti-Vietnam war movements shook the country and inspired young people to question authority. *Rolling Stone* magazine began publishing just in time for the Woodstock music festival in 1969, which cemented the hippie lifestyle in the American mind.

What did girls see from Barbie? By the late 1960s, she got "mod" clothes, following the miniskirt craze that came out of English designer Mary Quant's fashion house. Pairing the skirt with go-go boots, the Barbie Zokko! outfit was sold

ABOVE: Mattel celebrates forty-five years of Barbie fashion with a runway display featuring Barbies with clothes by designers such as Versace, Kate Spade, and Bob Mackie at the Mattel booth at Toy Fair in New York City, February 15, 2004.

in 1967. With its shimmery silver sleeveless top, bright blue-teal skirt, and splash-of-orange waistband, matched with orange dangly earrings, Barbie seemed to leave the 1950s far behind.

Then came the 1970s with the first Starbucks opening in Seattle, creating a common space for social meetings that would bloom everywhere in the country. Early personal computers, email, video games, and floppy discs hinted at the new future of technology. Cable television began reaching America's screens.

People talked about a sexual revolution changing society's attitudes toward marriage, divorce, and homosexuality. A "second wave" of the women's movement had brought feminism to the forefront, with calls for women's equality. Women were given the right to choose to have an abortion, birth control pills became more available, and the first test-tube baby was born.

Barbie leapt into the new freedom, capturing the spirit of the 1970s, with outfits like Flower Wower, with splotches of overlapping psychedelic flowers and bright green shoes.

ABOVE: Artist Andy Warhol displays his portrait of a Barbie doll in New York, on February 10, 1986.

ABOVE: A model displays an outfit including the iconic black-and-white zebra striped swimsuit, designed after the Number One Barbie, in the Barbie Runway Show during the 2009 Mercedes Benz Fashion Week in New York City, February 14, 2009.

ABOVE: Two models representing Barbie and Ken wear Kenneth Cole designs during the 2009 Mercedes Benz Fashion Week in New York City on February 14, 2009.

Maxi 'n Midi, with its belted coat of blue foil fabric and fluffy blue fur over a striped dress and knee-high boots; and Gypsy Spirit, with its pink chiffon blouse and blue-and-gold vest and skirt. Barbie even had a peasant blouse, while Ken had a fringed leather vest. For her sixteenth birthday, Barbie got a special-edition T-shirt-and-jeans outfit.

But Barbie maintained her glamorous tradition as well. In 1977, Superstar Barbie appeared. With her pink, satin low-cut dress, matching boa, strappy shoes, and star-shaped stand, Superstar Barbie had a teeth-flashing smile and higher-looking cheekbones. She was destined to be a bestseller for many years.

The 1980s saw Michael Jackson take over the music world with his album *Thriller*, as well as Madonna creating a sensation with her debut album. MTV was launched, as were McDonald's McNuggets. Children discovered Nintendo and *The Simpsons*. America continued to explore the universe with a successful space shuttle launch and a fatal mission by the *Columbia* to repair an orbiting satellite.

In form and fashion, Barbie took the lead in the 1980s, with an astronaut uniform that included a space helmet. Barbie and the Rockers met the "girl band" moment, hitting the stage with sparkles, shine, shimmer, and microphones. By her thirtieth birthday, in 1989, she was ready to celebrate her Pink Jubilee at New York's Lincoln Center. She had a full wardrobe for her growing list of careers, including a day-to-night outfit that could transform from a business suit to a glittering pink dress for a night on the town.

The 1980s also saw the first designer partnership. The Barbie brand collaborated with Oscar de la Renta to create

LEFT: Singer Cyndi Lauper poses with Barbie and Pooch the Pup at the unveiling of the "Ultimate Toy Catalog" at FAO Schwartz in New York City on October 10, 2001. The show benefited New Yorker's for Children's programs that help New York City children affected by the events of 9/11. RIGHT: Mattel and Ford join forces as both Barbie and the Mustang celebrate their 40th birthday at an event in Southern California on April 20, 1999.

four outfits in one package, which included three dresses for the red carpet and one pantsuit. And eight years after the first Barbie collector's convention, the 1988 Holiday Barbie started a tradition of glamorous collectible Barbie dolls.

Andy Warhol cemented the connection between Barbie and popular culture with his iconic image of Barbie's face. After Warhol painted Elvis, Marilyn Monroe, and Mickey Mouse, his muse, the jewelry designer called BillyBoy* (spelled with an asterisk), inspired him to paint Barbie.

Warhol had wanted to paint BillyBoy*, but he refused to cooperate and instead suggested Warhol paint BillyBoy*'s obsession—Barbie. Warhol used one of Billy Boy*'s tens of thousands of Barbie dolls as a model and called the painting *Portrait of BillyBoy**.

Later, BillyBoy* designed two Barbie dolls for Mattel, the Le Nouveau Theatre de la Mode doll, and the Feelin' Groovy doll. And for the first time, Mattel put the designer's name on the box. In 2014, BillyBoy* sold the Warhol Barbie painting for $1,161,780.

As Barbie continued her popularity in the 1990s, America was introduced to Amazon.com, Harry Potter, and the early

TOP: Some of the fifty blonde participants who entered a Barbie lookalike contest outside of Hotel Russell in London on January 17, 1991. BOTTOM: Adriana Karembeu, Ambassador of the French Red Cross, poses next to the 2003 Barbie jewelry collection where top jewelers got together to dress up a collection of Barbie dolls to be auctioned for the Red Cross in Paris, on December 18, 2003.

ABOVE: The Karl Lagerfeld Barbie doll, released in 2014, inspired by the designer's signature style, with elements borrowed from the Karl Lagerfeld line and Karl's iconic silhouette. The doll is dressed in a tailored black jacket, white high-collared men's shirt with French cuffs, black satin cravat, and fitted black jeans. Accessories include black fingerless gloves, a zippered handbag, and sunglasses.

web-based email service Hotmail. Britney Spears burst on the music scene, just as *Survivor* and *Buffy the Vampire Slayer* captivated television viewers.

For Barbie, the decade was marked by recognition of the amazing designers who continued to create her astonishing wardrobe, including Carol Spencer, Robert Best, Janet Goldblatt, Kitty Black-Perkins, Ann Driskill, Abbe Littleton, Monique Lhuillier, Anna Sui, and Cynthia Rowley, and the designers who, like Barbie, are recognizable by one name: Calvin, Cartier, Gucci, Versace, and Vera.

In 1990, Bob Mackie became the first of many famous designers to collaborate with the Barbie brand on a collector doll. His Gold Barbie featured five thousand hand-sewn golden sequins on a form-fitting, full-length gown with a crisscross bodice.

The 2000s saw hip-hop become part of the Rock and Roll Hall of Fame and a woman make two serious attempts at the presidency. Reality television and superhero films found popularity. Fashion often looked back to the '60s, '70s, and '80s, including velour tracksuits and tapered pants.

TOP: Close-up and profile views of the Karl Lagerfeld Barbie doll, released in 2014. **BOTTOM**: The late designer Karl Lagerfeld with the Barbie doll made in his likeness, in 2014.

For Barbie, more fashion collaborations were in store. A doll and shoe collection was created by Christian Louboutin. Fine jewelry called Barbie Rocks came from the design team of Layna and Alan Friedman. Coach got into Barbie's world with mini leather bags designed just for her. And when Barbie's foot was redesigned so that it could go to a flat position, Sophia Webster designed a line of flats for her new, flexible feet.

In 2009, for Barbie's fiftieth birthday, fifty-one designers created looks for Barbie's first-ever runway show, held at New York's Mercedes-Benz Fashion Week. From Donna Karan and Tommy Hilfiger, Diane von Furstenberg to Bob Mackie, the show opened with magnificent pink curtains drawing aside to reveal a model dressed as the Number One Barbie, in her original bathing suit, with a large blonde

ABOVE: Model, cover girl, and pageant-winner Corazon Ugalde Yellen Armenta poses in custom-made outfits modeled after Barbie fashions.

ponytail. The collection was described as "surreal" and included Ken in a black velvet jacket and jeans. The fabulous show, which drew screams of delight from mothers and daughters in the audience, moved on to a celebration at London Fashion Week that included the young designers Roksanda Ilincic and Danielle Scutt.

Barbie is captivating and compelling as a doll, and with her extraordinary fashions she becomes something more: an icon that invites imagination through not only playing her with or collecting her, but even *being* her.

Robert Best, senior design director at Mattel, is thoughtful about the history of Barbie fashion and his role in it. "I love having my name on dolls because I'm passionate about the doll, and I want to be part of the great legacy. I'm

part of the change, and the new guard. Collectors are aware of the history of Ruth Handler and Charlotte Johnson, and I'm the extension of that great tradition. We have younger designers who will take over from me. All of us are letting consumers know that we're listening."

One consumer and fan has brought Barbie design to real life. Corazon Ugalde Yellen Armenta, known simply as Cora, was born and raised in the Philippines where she didn't have a Barbie. She loved to play with fashion dolls, and after she came to the United States and had her daughter, she started buying Barbie dolls. Her passion for fashion was ignited! That was thirty-five years ago.

"I was a model and actress," Cora explains, "and did a beauty and fitness book, *Total Beauty in Life, the Natural*

ABOVE: Young models celebrating with designer Bettina Liano on the runway at the fashion launch for Barbie by Bettina Liano in Melbourne, Australia, on September 21, 2005.

Way. So, I loved Barbie because she was the ultimate fashion model."

Cora, a model and cover girl, became Mrs. Philippines 2018, and she competed for Mrs. Asia 2018. She's been in print and television commercials for Pepsi, Macy's, Western Airlines, and more, and she has modeled all over the world. In the 1990s, she modeled for many designers, including Lanvin and Yves Saint Laurent. She's also been an actress on television and on stage. Cora was dubbed a Living Doll Barbie after modeling several life-size Barbie fashions through the years for Barbie Conventions' fashion shows! As Cora says, "I feel like I did everything too, lots of careers and experiences, like Barbie." Cora has even had her face used to make a sculpt for an Asian mannequin for several department stores in the United States.

Cora founded the Beverly Hills Barbie Club but keeps her collection of more than a thousand Barbie dolls, as well as other dolls, in her Las Vegas home. She loves the vintage Barbie dolls and the classic haute couture, and has great memories of meeting designers Carol Spencer and Carlyle Nuera, who is Filipino.

Cora believes Barbie will be popular for "generations and generations," because mothers like her pass on their love of the doll to their children and grandchildren.

Cora says, "I love that Barbie can do anything and has so many careers. She's an American icon."

ABOVE: In New York City, models pose during Mercedez-Benz Fashion Week at Barbie's Dream Closet, where fans could step into one of several "closets" and, through augmented reality, virtually try on various Barbie outfits, in Lincoln Center at the David Rubenstein Atrium on February 11, 2012.

ABOVE: Barbie doll look-a-likes prepare to embark on a tour around the UK where they will meet thousands of fans. The ten real-life Barbies were all set to launch the country's biggest-ever Barbie event, at the Woolworth's store in London, on October 19, 2000.

Lisa McKnight, senior vice president and general manager for the Barbie brand at Mattel, is in charge of the Barbie lifestyle—everything that is Barbie around the world. If that sounds like a fun job, McKnight's quick smile seems to confirm that it is. Her office is a small museum of Barbie products. There is even a full-size surfboard, with Barbie's face covering the midsection, leaning against the wall.

As the mother of two teenage daughters, McKnight has seen the phenomenon that is her job on an up-close and personal basis from home to work and stretching back to her childhood. "I loved Barbie when I was young, and I played with her along with my younger sister. I was fascinated with being the older girl and played out being a babysitter because a babysitter could drive a car and have a boyfriend," McKnight laughs. "I also liked being a teacher, and I was an athlete. I played soccer, so Malibu Barbie was a favorite."

ABOVE: The Barbie Fashion Designer Collection Launch by Bettina Liano fashion parade in Australia starred twenty-five young girls, on September 21, 2005.

McKnight oversees a massive workspace in the Handler Building in El Segundo. The open floor plan has been transformed into a warren of cubicles filled with creative people who are working on one of the many aspects of the Barbie brand. But unlike other cubicle-type office spaces, the Barbie work area is a visual carnival of all things Barbie. Every sort of Barbie doll, her relatives and friends, vintage and new, partial and assembled, along with accessories and playthings galore, can be seen around the room. Employees have decorated their workspaces, including the curtains that cover some of the cubicle entrances, desks, and shelves, with their own sense of fun, play, and aesthetics. You get the sense that everyone not only loves Barbie, but they love how they're adding to her world. And they're on a mission.

It was around 2008, McKnight explains when Mattel "honed in on the notion that through Barbie, a girl can be

ABOVE: Ten-year-old Olga Bagiotas from Prahan, Australia, with Barbie on the catwalk during the Barbie by Bettina Liano Designer Collection Star Search casting session in Australia, on July 7, 2005.

whatever she wants to be. We've become maniacally focused on why Ruth Handler created Barbie. She knew there was a dream gap for girls, and there still is."

McKnight and her team are looking at what Barbie inspires and enables that is beyond the doll. "She's more than a doll," McKnight says, "but the doll started it all, and we've extended and expanded the brand."

The goal is to help girls believe they can be anything, and McKnight understands how relevant that idea is to the world today. "The culture and society embrace Barbie, and Barbie is also part of the culture. We're showing girls Shero and Inspiring Women dolls." She takes a Frida Kahlo and a Katherine Johnson doll off her shelf. Looking at the great artist and the great mathematician, she says, "If you can't see it, you can't be it."

McKnight adds that the fun in the brand is that it is timeless. Just as when Barbie first appeared, girls enjoy the setup time for imaginary play. "Watching my two daughters set up a world," McKnight says, "I can see them take cues from the product lines. The Dreamhouse is a cornerstone, and then they play out stories from television or school. They try on different voices. It reminds me of my time playing Barbie. The play pattern is timeless."

Mattel's #DadsWhoPlayBarbie campaign is a perfect example of art imitating life, and McKnight's own home is no exception. She adds that her husband is a great father of daughters and gets involved in Barbie play too. She loves the line from the brand campaign: "Time spent in her imaginary world is an investment in her real world." McKnight adds, "It's also a way to help them shape their future selves."

LEFT: American actress Ever Carradine brings the Barbie Art & Craft Studio playset as a donation to Motorola's Third Annual Holiday Party to Benefit Toys for Tots at The Highlands in Hollywood, California, on December 6, 2001. **RIGHT**: Journalist Deborah Norville poses with four Barbie dolls at the at the 40th Anniversary Gala for "The Barbie Doll" at the Waldorf Astoria Hotel in New York City, on February 7, 1999.

What keeps her culturally relevant? McKnight says it's the power of the girls who have the experience of play in their hands and minds. McKnight explains, "So long as girls want to imagine and discover the world around them, and role-play, there will be the play pattern for Barbie. There's this wonderful open-endedness to Barbie. She's a canvas for storytelling."

McKnight also understands that Barbie is a physical toy, and that aspect of her has to keep pace with culture to stay relevant. She has to reflect the world, and that has been a major push at the brand. Barbie is more accessible and inclusive than ever before. She has diversity in her race, body type, facial characteristics, hair, skin tone, and clothes. Soon, a Barbie that is differently abled will add a new real-world dimension. Her accessories, which range from adaptive devices to an open-plan house, are specially designed for this series.

Barbie has evolved from a doll to a lifestyle brand. McKnight explains that girls can experience Barbie at every point in their day. They can wake up on Barbie sheets in Barbie pajamas, brush their teeth with a Barbie toothbrush, slip on a branded backpack and sneakers, and at bath time find many Barbie products to use. Barbie appears on screens as well, with her Netflix show *Barbie's Dreamhouse Adventures*, a YouTube channel, and a variety of apps.

According to McKnight, "Barbie is as relevant today as sixty years ago. Most toys have three- to five-year life cycles, so she is unique in the toy industry. Barbie stands the test of time. Everyone has their Barbie story."

LEFT: Designer Bob Mackie poses with the new Liberty Barbie Doll that he designed, on May 24, 2000. **RIGHT:** American businesswoman Jill Barad, CEO of Mattel from 1997 to 2000, poses with a collection of oversized Barbie dolls, on January 1, 2000. **FOLLOWING:** Meet the new crew. The Barbie Fashionistas are the most diverse and inclusive fashion doll line. Designed to better reflect the world that girls see today, the line features a variety of skin tones, eye colors, hairstyles, body types, and fashions.

chapter 7

GOING GLOBAL

Barbie has been a global phenomenon for six decades. The Barbie experience, grown from Ruth Handler's belief that there is a better way to express fashion play—and that little girls want to play at being big girls—is universal. From Asia to the Middle East, from Australia to Alaska, you can circle the globe today and find girls and boys letting their imaginations build new adventures for the many toys that are part of the Barbie brand.

But unlike sixty years ago, there is a new world of technology connecting Barbie fans across continents and oceans. No matter your language or your country, no matter whether you live in a big city or a remote village, you are invited to share in Barbie's ever-changing world.

Shortly after the first Barbie went on sale, Dell Comics began a series of comic books called *Barbie and Ken*. Readers were invited to travel along as the duo went to Europe,

played tennis, made an appearance onstage, and had other adventures. There was also the bimonthly *Barbie* magazine, with features like how to grow a salad, babysitting, and making a paper dress.

The magazine also had a series on girls around the world with titles like, "If You Were an Irish Girl" and "If You Were an Israeli Girl." Through the magazine, girls learned that Barbie's father was George Roberts, and her mother was Margaret. She had a sister named Skipper, and Midge had a brother named Albert.

There was also a Barbie fan club, which grew exponentially throughout Barbie's first decade, without the advantage of social media! But as the Internet has taken hold, there are chat rooms dedicated to the Barbie brand, and websites that let fans and collectors broadcast their ideas for Barbie, her friends, her fashions, and her larger world of houses and accessories.

OPPOSITE: Mattel features the *Legally Blonde 2* collection at the 2003 Toy Fair in New York City on February 16, 2003.

Today, Barbie has a Facebook page with about fifteen million followers, two Instagram accounts (@Barbie, and @barbiestyle) with more than three million followers, a Twitter account (@Barbie), and uses the hashtag #YouCanBeAnything. Her YouTube channel, which has six million subscribers, hosts Barbie's vlog, everything that is Dreamtopia, and more. Overall, Barbie has more than twenty million social followers, and is the number-one toy brand in social conversation!

And there's more. Films are in the works, the streaming channel Netflix is in its eighth season of *Barbie Life in the Dreamhouse*, with a new show, *Barbie's Dreamhouse Adventures*, in its second year, and Barbie is a video game hero, available for interactive imagining through gaming devices.

All these ways to view, learn about, and interact with Barbie have given her 99 percent brand awareness. She is an enormous presence throughout the world.

One of Barbie's most exciting global events was her exhibition at the Musée des Arts Décoratifs at the Palais du Louvre in Paris, France. Under triple arches, at the top of a broad marble staircase, a solid pink wall announced "Barbie." Inside, seven hundred Barbie dolls were displayed. The innovative arrangements of dolls showed all of Barbie's more than two dozen hair colors, her fourteen skin tones, and her new shapes and sizes.

Anne Monier, curator of the Louvre's Toy department, told National Public Radio, "Beauty is also about diversity. And today, you cannot give a child one doll and say, this is a beautiful doll. You need to show the child different models of beauty so that they can pick the one that they want to identify with."

The museum included works from their collection of dolls and gowns, as well as works by contemporary artists, and a full spectrum of media exhibits that show how the world has changed during Barbie's six decades.

Perhaps there's no better testimony to Barbie's global

ABOVE: More than seven hundred Barbie dolls are displayed during the exhibition "Barbie, Life of an Icon" at the Museum of Decorative Arts as part of Paris Fashion Week, on March 9, 2016.

reach than the dedication of fans across the globe. A few collectors have caught the world's attention. Devoted to Barbie in their own special way, they discover their creative expression and their love for helping others through her inspiration.

Jian Yang lives in the Bartley neighborhood of Singapore. In his gleaming white apartment, thousands of Barbie dolls, neatly lined up, sit on the shelves that cover his living room walls. They frame his television with a kaleidoscope of color as an entertaining reminder of his fascination with Barbie.

Jian has been in the advertising business for nearly twenty years, and for all that time, and longer, Barbie dolls have captivated him.

Jian's introduction to Barbie came in 1984, when he was five years old. He couldn't read the names on the presents under the Christmas tree, so he opened a present meant for his two-year-old sister. It was a Great Shape Barbie in a turquoise leotard and matching headband, and he loved it. His second doll was a hit with him too. "I got Dream Glow Barbie," Jian says. "She had

ABOVE: Collector and artist Jian Yang from Singapore poses with a small selection of Barbie dolls from his huge collection of more than twelve thousand dolls sourced from fifty different countries.

Going Global | 147

ABOVE: An assortment of Jian Yang's fashions that he creates while traveling using various forms of paper products, including toilet paper, napkins, and tissue.

glow-in-the-dark stars on her dress," Jian remembers, "so I'd crawl under the bed and watch her glow."

G.I. Joes, Transformers, and other more traditional "boy" toys were what Jian often played with, but Barbie represented something different for him. Jian explains, "As a teenager, the boy toys went away, but I kept my Barbies. I never really played imaginary games or made up stories with Barbie. To me, she was an iconic illustration. She was like a drawing that came to life." He started getting an allowance in his teens and used the money to buy more dolls and clothes.

Jian does not like to call himself a "collector," since his incentive for getting dolls is not to complete a certain series and he doesn't buy dolls to sell them. "I've always been a very private collector. I always just figured I was a boy who played with toys," Jian says, "and one of those toys happened to be Barbie. I'm very visual, so when I see a doll I like, I decide if I want it." On that basis, Jian has amassed twelve thousand dolls, the second-largest collection in the world.

And he has discovered a wonderfully creative side to himself—the creation of Barbie clothes from tissue, toilet paper, and napkins. Jian's paper Barbie wardrobe is fragile, astonishing, and mesmerizing. It's difficult to imagine how he could create such intricate dresses, hats, and flowers with such delicate material.

As for how he started making these fabulous designs, Jian said, "I was sent to Colombo, Sri Lanka, by my company. I stayed at this big hotel on the edge of Colombo by the sea. There was nothing around the hotel, and nothing to do, and I was stuck there every night. One day, I bought a Barbie doll in Colombo. As I sat in the hotel, I realized I had some tape in my toiletry bag and some manicure scissors, and of course, there was toilet paper in the bathroom. So, I sat on the toilet and made a rosette. I always liked to fiddle with stuff, so I randomly rolled the toilet paper and thought, 'Hey, a rose.'" That was Jian's first creation, but he wasn't satisfied with it, so he made another.

For the next two weeks, he made a rosette every night. He put the best one on Instagram, and it got a good response, so he made more. Soon he branched out to

dresses, everything from sleek strapless evening gowns to a dirndl-skirted party dress, and imaginative hats, all made from white tissue.

Jian has a rule: he only does tissue creations when he travels. He says, "It's an interesting way to document my travel because I use paper from where I am." He is starting to use napkins from restaurants he visits. And he jokes, "As a homeowner with lots of expenses, I need to save money, so that's why I use hotel toilet paper."

A friend of Jian's, who was an editor at the Singapore edition of *Nylon* magazine, wrote an article on Jian's paper Barbie dresses and published it without telling him. International media picked up the article, and then, as Jian says, "It went crazy." He was particularly pleased that his "toilet paper creations" were featured in Italian *Vogue*.

Jian still buys dolls. His new Barbie dolls arrive weekly in Amazon boxes. He's also listed in Asia Book of Records for having the largest collection in Asia. Why is he still

ABOVE: Collector and artist Jian Yang poses with a vintage Number One blonde ponytail Barbie doll in front of his pristine collection at his home in Singapore.

amassing his dolls? Jian explains, "I've been in advertising for a long time, and in advertising you have to be in tune with trends and pop culture. I see Barbie as a pop culture icon. For instance, the Misty Copeland doll introduced me to her story. I did my research, and now I'm deeply knowledgeable about a pop culture icon who's indicative of celebrity. Barbie tells the world's story through one medium, which is the toy."

Jian sees Barbie as a doorway into different parts of the culture. "Barbie is for older fans, like with the Barbra Streisand doll," Jian explains, "and for children with the Nutcracker movie, and then there's Ladies of the '80s for the middle-age group. As an advertising guy, that intrigues me." Even though Jian travels for his work and has seen a lot of the world, he believes Barbie lets him see even more.

"I'm a Scorpio, so I'm quite extreme," explains Jian. "And if I like something, I fall deeply in love with it. With Barbie I see all the consumer touch-points and how a market is built. I like the creation of Barbie's fictional universe, which isn't bound by stereotypes that might be held about people in the Middle East, or Americans, or Asians. I'll never get rid of my dolls. Barbie will always be that icon. She's forever, certainly as a part of history."

How many stories of Barbie are there? In Australia, a Barbie fan is answering that question on her own YouTube channel.

ABOVE: A child model walks down the runway during the "Barbie Featuring the Pink Dolls" portion of the Macy's Passport Gala to Benefit HIV/AIDS Research and Awareness in Santa Monica, California, on September 30, 2004.

Grace Mulgrew is twelve years old, but her love of Barbie started when she was only three. Her bright eyes sparkle as she remembers a Barbie doll as "almost the first toy that I got." She liked to play a game she called "Hello" with her parents. The game started with Grace having her Barbie say hello, and then having a conversation with her mom or dad. Little did she or her parents know that Grace's Barbie would become much more than a beloved toy.

At home in suburban Melbourne, Australia, Grace has a drawer full of more than a hundred Barbie dolls. She always liked to act out stories as she played by herself or her cousins, who would come to visit. She loved the idea of acting, and at six years old, she liked to watch YouTube videos. "I thought

it would be cool to see one of my own videos up there with the other Barbie videos." One day, she combined her two interests, and asked her father to videotape her as her Barbie went on a tour of Grace's Anneliese dollhouse.

In the video, Grace pretends to be her blonde Barbie as she shows viewers what's in the refrigerator, how the oven opens, the airplane where Barbie's mother and sister sleep, and the upstairs of the dollhouse, where Barbie takes a shower fully clothed, complete with water sounds. Grace talks almost nonstop, a little girl's voice showing the grown-up world of her house. Throughout, you see Grace holding Barbie and occasionally glimpse Grace's face. As her father, Greg says, it was an amateur effort.

ABOVE: A collection of Barbie dolls from the exhibit "Barbie the Icon," held at MUDEC (Museo delle Culture) in Milan, Italy, on February 10, 2016.

ABOVE: A canceled postage stamp celebrating Classic Toys from Australia with an image of a vintage 1962 Red Flare Barbie doll, circa 2009.

Greg put the video up on YouTube, and neither he nor Grace looked at it again. Then, about nine months later, Grace's cousin called with startling news. He told Grace that her video on YouTube was really popular. Grace said, "No, you have the wrong video." But when she looked on YouTube she found that her video had nine million views! Grace and Greg couldn't believe it, so they made another video.

In the second video, Grace pretends to be Barbie as a mother of twins taking them on a cruise ship with Ken. They have various adventures, including falling into the water, going swimming, and getting lost on a small sand island that Greg built in the swimming pool he used as a "set." Unfortunately, the sand made the water brown, and some fans complained that Barbie and her family were swimming in dirty water! But the video got even more views than the first one. As she acted out Barbie skits to upload on YouTube, Grace had become an actress, just as she had dreamed of.

In those first videos, you can see Grace holding the dolls, and here and there her mother and sister in the background. But Greg said, "Kids didn't care about the quality [of the video]. They cared about the story. We planned out ahead what was going to happen with Barbie, but it wasn't scripted. It was like the camera wasn't even there." After about ten videos, Greg started using a green screen, so Grace's hand and arm didn't show as Barbie was moved around.

After six years, Grace has had more than a billion total views, and she has nearly one-and-a-half million subscribers to her YouTube channel, *Grace's World.* Grace's "Hello" game is still the basis for her stories, which are about what she sees in everyday life. She also has about two hundred ideas from fans who would like to see her act out the stories they have imagined. Grace says, "I really like acting and making videos. I also love shopping in clothing stores." Grace has done a lot of traveling in the past year, to California, New York, Chicago, and Honolulu, and to Disney World and Disneyland.

Grace's favorite Barbie dolls are the Dreamhouse dolls. "I remember the day I got Barbie's Life in the Dreamhouse doll. She brings back lots of memories of how much I loved her when I first got her, how excited I was. When I'd get

TOP: Grace Mulgrew with her collection of Barbie dolls, 2019. **MIDDLE**: A screen shot from Episode 179, "The Karate Master," from Grace's World. **BOTTOM**: A screen shot from Episode 183, "The Imaginary Friend," from Grace's World.

barbiestyle ✔ • Follow
Bergdorf Goodman

barbiestyle The amazing @iris.apfel is truly a one-of-a-kind! She's one of my role models so it's an honor to be here at @bergdorfs to celebrate her new book, #AccidentalIcon! 📚 #IrisApfelxBG #barbie #barbiestyle

Load more comments

kath1889 @soozee_2407

خیلی عالی بود لطفا پیج منم دیدن کنی ma2shop.ir

cootandbella yes please!!! how do i order??🖤🖤🖤🖤🖤

cootandbella @cootandbella asking for my momma!!! (pet parent, ya know!)

franassiss @alexandra_saboia_ 😎

danredz @ferltn

a_unicorn_gar Ей не идут очки

essteiner @knowledgeisforcutting

♡ ⎯ ⬆

79,473 likes

MARCH 15

home from school, she was the first thing I picked up. She had real eyelashes, and she was fully posable, and so was Ken. That was important to making videos." Barbie's friends, like Teresa, Summer, and Raquel, also became a big part of Grace's videos. Mainly, Grace imagines Barbie as a businesswoman. Sometimes she's married with children, and sometimes she's a princess with a magic wand.

Grace thinks Barbie will "definitely be forever, 'cause she'll change and there'll always be new ideas, and young girls will always want to play with her and dress her up." What will Grace be when she grows up? "I'd still love to be an actress, but if that doesn't work, I also think about being a child psychologist because I like kids and I'd like to help them with problems. Sometimes I act out that Barbie is a therapist. And lots of times, I play with Barbie as a movie star in a limousine."

"We can see through Grace's videos how well Barbie is doing, and how kids are latching on to it every day as they come on to her channel," Greg says. Last January, he quit his job as a computer programmer so he could work on Grace's videos full-time. Thanks to Barbie, Greg and Grace have not only a rare father-daughter bond, but they have a business that relies on Grace's creativity and the doll she has always loved. Grace is not alone in entertaining fans through social media.

In Los Angeles, California, another fan shares her own love of Barbie. Azusa Yakamoto has large dark eyes, long blond hair with straight-cut bangs, and porcelain skin. She's thirty-six and was born in Japan, where she had fashion dolls as a child, but Barbies were difficult to find. She finally received a Barbie lunchbox when she was fifteen years old. She says, "I was so unlucky when I was little, because I couldn't get a Barbie. But because of that, I never saw the doll as a little kid's toy."

Azusa loved her lunchbox, which looked "like cool American pop culture." She loved pop fashion and the color pink. Soon she was using the lunchbox as a purse. Around this time, Azusa became an exchange student in the little

---

ABOVE: Barbie's official Instagram page, @barbiestyle, has more than 2 million followers. In this post from March 15, 2018, the Iris Apfel Barbie doll, modeled after the dynamic fashion icon, poses with Barbie, celebrating the release of her new book, *Iris Apfel: Accidental Icon*.

 barbiestyle ✔ • Follow
Marciano Art Foundation

barbiestyle Made it to
@marcianoartfoundation for the perfect
picture opp. The #KusamaxMAF exhibit
"With All My Love For The Tulips, I Pray
Forever (2011)" has me seeing spots! 🖤
#YayoiKusama #MAF #barbie
#barbiestyle

Load more comments

erica9876543210 @anoma_andy

barbie_fotos_anto

creativewithdolls Love her art sooo! 😍

♡   💬   ⬆️   🔖

31,385 likes

AUGUST 30

TOP LEFT: Image from Barbie's Instagram page, @barbiestyle, shows Barbie, Ashley Graham, and Ibtihaj Muhammad dolls at the *Glamour Magazine* Women of the Year Awards on November 13, 2017. **TOP RIGHT**: Barbie at Christian Siriano's show during New York Fashion Week on September 9, 2017. **BOTTOM**: Barbie visiting the Yayoi Kusama exhibit at the Marciano Art Foundation in Los Angeles on August 30, 2017.

town of Bluffton, Indiana, where she lived on a farm for a year. She was delighted to be able to start collecting Barbie dolls. She says, "I bought whatever I liked. My host family had kids who were fourteen and eleven and had already stopped playing with Barbie dolls. They made fun of my interest. But I didn't know why, because I didn't think Barbie was for kids."

Azusa returned to Japan, where a rare and terrible disease struck her. She had surgery and was in the hospital for two months. When she recovered, she started selling Barbie-brand adult clothes, and she bought more Barbie dolls. She was working hard in Japan and saving money to move to the United States. One of the reasons she wanted to move was that Barbie-brand items were very expensive in Japan.

When Azusa was thirty she got a student visa to come

to America. She got a manicure license and started to do nail art. "I started designing Barbie nails to match Barbie fashions," Azusa explains.

Today she's married, living in Los Angeles, and has about 250 dolls, but it is Barbie-brand adult clothes and purses that make up the bulk of her collection. She has about 170 Barbie T-shirts, plus Barbie sweaters and sweatshirts, and more than five dozen purses. She's still collecting more clothes than dolls. "I wear the clothes every day. That is my wardrobe," she laughs. "I only own Barbie shirts."

Manicuring is Azusa's main business, along with a YouTube channel called *Azusa Barbie*. The videos range from how to cook pink pasta, corn dogs, or popcorn, to watching Azusa's morning routine in her Barbie-themed apartment. She has used five shades of pink to paint every room and

ABOVE: Barbie blogger and collector Azusa Sakamoto—also known as Azusa Barbie—poses in her Barbie-themed home, which she has turned into a Barbie shrine, in West Hollywood, on December 12, 2018.

ABOVE: Azusa Yakamoto's real-life Barbie dream house contains all things pink. Azusa is shown in her West Hollywood home on December 29, 2017.

filled the apartment with Barbie-brand items like pillows, teacups, and posters.

There are also plenty of do-it-yourself Barbie decorations, like the slatted blinds, a cabinet, and even the refrigerator. Azusa explains, "I love DIY! I'm not just buying. I like creating by myself. When I think of something that I want with Barbie, if Mattel doesn't sell it, then I make it. I paint everything—walls, cabinets, floors—so it looks like Barbie's house. That's what Barbie tells us: we can be anything. Anything is possible. That's Barbie's attitude, so that's why I do it myself."

Azusa's YouTube channel started only recently, but she's up to more than 80,000 subscribers. She's hoping it will grow more to help her achieve her life's goal, which has

to do with her illness as a teenager. She still has the rare disease and has had six surgeries because of it. "That's what made me feel that I should do whatever I want to do," Azusa says, "because I learned early that life is fragile. I want to help kids, to do kids' nails, to donate Barbies. I want to help a million kids who are sick or poor."

Barbie's magic captured Azusa's attention in Japan, where Barbie was first made. She brought her dreams, and her love of the doll, halfway around the world, and her devotion to Barbie is stronger than ever. "I think Barbie's forever," Azusa says, "because she's not just a kid's fashion doll. She's a fashion item. She's not just a popular toy for one generation. She is totally a part of culture, and I love her."

ABOVE: Azusa Yakamoto, Kii Arens, Neon Music, and Posh attend an art-inspired launch for the collaboration of PUMA and Barbie as they come together for a collaboration around PUMA'S suede 50th anniversary in Los Angeles, California, on December 06, 2018.

ABOVE: Inside Azusa Yakamoto's Barbie-themed home in West Hollywood, California. Her collection includes dolls, artwork, a Barbie-themed guitar, bags, pillows, curtains, and all things pink. **FOLLOWING:** To celebrate the opening of their store in Miami Beach, Florida, Alchemist—a retailer whose mission is to bring together the synergetic world of fashion, design, and architecture—partnered with to exhibit a Barbie retrospective. The installation featured ten life-sized Barbie dolls dressed in custom Chrome Hearts clothing and jewelry with hair styled by celebrity hairstylist Oribe Canales, on April 9, 2010.

chapter 8

THE MAGIC OF BARBIE

Barbie has fans of all ages, races, and genders. They live all over the world, and their affection for Barbie is enduring. But can it last forever? The best answer comes from the children and parents, the fans and collectors who continue to be inspired, delighted, and empowered by Barbie. Here's a wonderful example from one mother and daughter.

Kara Norman's ten-year-old daughter, Kennedy, was excited to try the simple experiments in her new chemistry set. She had a great idea. Why not use the lab set to create a pretend lab/classroom with her I Can Be . . . Teacher Barbie doll? She used other Barbie dolls as students and was soon using her teacher Barbie to explain the experiments to her "class." The students raised their hands, with help from Kennedy, of course. Kennedy, wearing protective goggles and engrossed in her pretend job, wrote out her pH test results on a whiteboard.

Kara, who runs Empower Her, Inc., a nonprofit to empower women and girls, thinks it is important to get girls interested in STEM (science, technology, engineering, and math fields). Kara was delighted to see Kennedy take a science kit and turn it into an imaginary world, which gave her an idea.

At Kennedy's next birthday party, Kara based her theme on Barbie's "I Can Be" line of career dolls. Kennedy's friends came dressed as what they wanted to be when they grew up. Kara says, "I didn't stop there. I had someone come in and do a robotics demonstration with the girls and boys, and at the end of the party they built their own robots."

The genius of Barbie has always been that she is what her fans make her. Absent the ingredient of human imagination, Barbie is just a doll. She is simply pieces of molded plastic in the shape of a woman. She is a caricature, or a toy-sized mannequin.

OPPOSITE: Barbara Handler—daughter of Ruth and Elliot Handler, and namesake for the Barbie doll—poses with a Barbie doll after placing her hands in cement that will adorn the sidewalk at the Egyptian Theatre in Hollywood, California, in an event designed to honor Barbie, on November 13, 2002

But her creator, Ruth Handler, understood the depth of children's imaginations. She had seen it in her daughter, along with something more. She saw the deep desire of children to play and pretend about the world they will enter.

Barbie, with her ageless features, is also timeless. To one four-year-old, she may be a dress-up doll, to another, a doll to act out her dreams. But to an adolescent, Barbie can take on different roles in different worlds, including those of fantasy. She also invites adults to fantasize. With her ever-

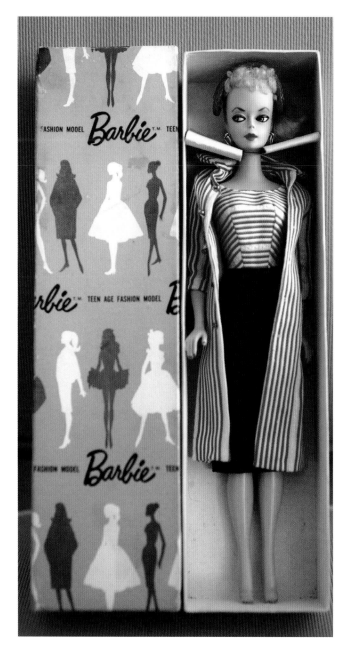

changing fashions and, more recently, her broad selection of face sculpts, skin tones, body types, and hair choices, she offers her fans the chance to imagine more than ever before.

This is Barbie's magic. Her ability to come to life in our minds, and especially in the minds of girls, creates a rich synergy that has a power of its own. Childhood longing for and curiosity about adult life is universal and never-ending. Every generation looks forward from the safety of childhood play to the challenges of adult life. Barbie lets her fans practice their future, enter their future, and believe in their future, at the same time that they delight in playing with her. Or as Mattel says, "When a girl plays with Barbie she imagines everything she can become."

For sixty years, girls have opened their first Barbie and recognized a friend and companion. Barbie has helped out at lemonade stands, gone on vacation with girls' families, and been seen in countless home videos and photographs. Girls have imagined her in jobs well beyond those suggested by Mattel. She has also turned magical as a fairy, witch, and countless creatures known only to the girls who make them up.

The doll also opens up the opportunity for mother-daughter play in ways that are far more broad and interesting than baby dolls. Barbie dolls encourage artistic play, from sewing or decorating clothes, to designing houses and décor, to styling the doll's hair. They open up new dialogues. Moms might come home from the office to find themselves talking about their day with Barbie, their daughter's avatar who also has an office job. Girls talk and act through Barbie in just the kind of expansive play pattern that Ruth had envisioned.

Girls also have a unique attachment to their Barbie dolls that Ruth had seen from the start. She knew the doll would become part of the child, and a way for girls to see their dreams and goals through the doll. She had watched her own daughter play with paper dolls in the same way. She had a strong sense that if she could get the doll into the marketplace, consumers would do the rest.

As we know by now, Barbie is not just for girls.

Stanley Colorite's smile is as bright as his pink suit jacket and matching shoes. He's forty-six years old and the

ABOVE: A vintage 1959 Barbie doll dressed in Roman Holiday attire is displayed during the 2006 Barbie Doll Collectors Convention, where hundreds of dealers and collectors buy, sell, and trade Barbie dolls and accessories, in Los Angeles, California, on July 26, 2006.

biggest Barbie collector in the United States, with more than five thousand dolls. All his dolls are taken out of the boxes and put in air-sealed containers. He also has ten Dreamhouses, five thousand fashions from 1959 to 2018, and fifteen cars.

His house in Florida is a joyous, colorful display of all things Barbie. Dolls line the walls in neat rows. As Stanley says, "It's nice to wake up every day and have beauty around you."

Stanley's interest was sparked by his mother, who was also a collector. He started out with Jem and the Holograms and G.I. Joe, but in 1992, tragedy struck. His mother died in a fire, and in memory of her, he kept her collection going. By 1997, he was a Barbie collector. "I went to the Salvation Army," Stanley says, "and bought the 1992 Happy Holiday Barbie. She was my first." He also bought the dentist Barbie, which had jointed elbows and a button to push that made

TOP: Kitturah Westenhouser, collector and author of *The Story of Barbie*, poses with part of her Barbie collection. **BOTTOM**: Kitty Stuart—owner of Kitty's Collectables, one of the largest vintage Barbie doll dealerships—poses in 1997 with an "artist doll" by David Escobedo that is sculpted in Kitty's likeness, next to some of her thousands of Barbie dolls. Kitty is wearing a "Barbie at the Beach" hand-painted jacket by popular designer Tony Alamo.

TOP: Bettina Dorfman, the owner of the world's largest Barbie collection, poses in front of some of her fifteen thousand dolls. **BOTTOM LEFT**: Bettina Dorfman poses with a vintage Number One Barbie from 1959. **BOTTOM RIGHT**: Not just a collector, Bettina Dorfman is also a doll doctor and runs a Barbie hospital from her home, where she repairs broken dolls sent to her from all over the world.

her talk. He liked that she could cross her legs, and that her wrists moved like Jem's. He liked to play with the dolls that sparked his sense of fun and his imagination.

Stanley's mother's dolls were naked, so he bought an identification book and started buying clothes that went with them. He also went to doll shows and spent hours in the Barbie aisle at Toys "R" Us. His mother had dolls from the 1970s that she bought at flea markets, and he managed to dress them all.

The oldest doll Stanley has is the Number Three Barbie. His collection goes from 1960 to the present. Stanley says, "I buy it all. I only buy Barbies. I also have a massive Jem collection, but my main thing is Barbie. I also have every Midge, Teresa, PJ, Stacey, and Skipper." Stanley says his boyfriend is a Ken collector, and he has every Ken ever made. "I buy all the dolls I miss from my childhood," Stanley says. "I look for Halloween Barbies and Valentine and Birthday. Collectors are looking for what they're missing."

How does Stanley find new dolls for his collection? All sorts of ways. He shared one example from 2001. "FAO Schwarz went out of business in Michigan, where I'm from. I had a lady who was general manager of FAO. She sold the window displays of the Bob Mackie Barbies. I got them all for fifty dollars each, with the boxes that said 'FAO Schwarz exclusive.'"

These days, Stanley is a designer for a hospice that has a thrift store, where he works on displays. He also helps at the PAWS animal shelter thrift store and designs dolls to raise money for animals and for hospice.

Stanley's not actively adding to his collection right now, although he plans to get the sixtieth Anniversary Barbie. He's also hoping that the Ladies of the '80s collection will be expanded to include Tina Turner, Pat Benatar, and Madonna. Stanley thinks Barbie is forever because she's outlasted every other toy. He says, "Barbie would live on even if she was discontinued, because of secondary markets like eBay. There are so many Barbies out in the world. She'll always be around."

And last, but certainly not least, there's one collector who outshines them all.

Bettina Dorfmann lives in Dusseldorf, Germany, which straddles the Rhine River and is a city known for its fashion industry and art scene. For twenty-five years, Bettina—with her broad smile and long, straight, natural blonde hair—has amassed the largest-known collection of Barbie dolls in the world, according to *Guinness World Records 2011*, which recognized Bettina for owning fifteen thousand Barbie dolls.

Bettina's interest began at six years old with a blonde-haired Midge. "I played with the doll every day with my friends," Bettina remembers. "We could sew for the doll, and we could play all situations from our own life, from the television, or from other stories."

Bettina didn't start collecting until 1993. She had tried to give her childhood dolls to her daughter, who only wanted more modern dolls. Bettina realized that her dolls reminded her of her own childhood and her friends and birthdays and Christmas, when she would get new dolls. She realized something important and thought, *Barbie is a mirror of our own life!* Naturally, the first doll in her collection was a rare 1963 Midge doll.

After some years of collecting, Bettina started to repair Barbie dolls. She created her own Barbie clinic, the only one in Germany. Then she began work on a Barbie museum and started holding Barbie exhibitions. Her collection really began to grow at that time, because her exhibitions required a lot of dolls. She became such an expert that she has been called on to create reports for legal cases or insurance claims that involve the doll.

Bettina told the World Record Academy, "There's probably nothing I don't know about Barbie. It drives my husband crazy every time I come home with a new doll. When I tell him it's getting harder and harder to get the rare ones he laughs and says, 'That's because they are all here in the house!'"

Bettina says, "Everything about her—her clothes, hairstyles, makeup, sports, jobs, designer items, Hollywood glamour—are all things from our lives. And she is always up to date, including accessories, which are very important, and her jobs, like going from stewardess to pilot."

She adds, "Barbie is a mirror of our world. She is forever."

FOLLOWING: Barbie doll collector Tina Brettnacher presents some of her rarest and oldest dolls to celebrate Barbie's 60th birthday during an exhibition dedicated to Barbie at "La Nef des Jouets" in Soultz, France, which ran from March 9, to June 30, 2019.

Barbie et Ken en tenue de mariés
1963

BIBLIOGRAPHY

Many of the following books and articles were useful in writing this book, and serve as a resource guide for anyone interested in Barbie.

Abrams, Rachel. "Barbie Adds Curvy and Tall to Body Shapes." *New York Times.* January 28, 2016. https://www.nytimes.com/2016/01/29/business/barbie-now-in-more-shapes.html

Abrams, Rachel. "Mattel Aims to Reanimate Sales with Talking Barbie." *New York Times.* October 15, 2015. https://www.nytimes.com/2015/10/16/business/mattel-aims-to-reanimate-sales-with-interactive-barbie.html

Abrams, Rachel. "Mattel Takes a Risk, with Barbie and Bugs." *New York Times.* December 28, 2015. https://www.nytimes.com/2015/12/28/business/mattel-takes-a-risk-with-barbie-and-bugs.html

Alexander, Hilary. "Barbie celebrates 50th birthday with her very own fashion show." *The Telegraph.* February 14, 2009.

Augustyniak, J. Michael. *The Barbie Doll Boom: Identification and Values.* Collector Books, 1996.

Augustyniak, J. Michael. *Barbie Doll Around the World 1964–2007*: Identification & Values. Collector Books, 2007.

Augustyniak, J. Michael. *Barbie Doll Photo Album 1959 to 2009.* Collector Books, 2010.

Augustyniak, J. Michael. *Collector's Encyclopedia of Barbie Doll Collector's Editions.* Collector Books, 2007.

Barbielist Holland. "1959–2014 Fifty-five Years Big Changes of the Barbie Doll (Part I)." BarbielistHolland.wordpress.com (blog). October 18, 2014. https://barbielistholland.wordpress.com/2014/10/18/1959-2014-fityfive-years-big-changes-of-the-barbie-doll-part-i/.

Barrowclough, Anne. "Rolf Hausser: Creator of the Bild Lilli Doll." FondationTanagra.com. n.d. http://www.fondationtanagra.com/en/article/rolf-hausser-the-creator-of-the-bild-lilli-doll/page/lilli-in-america.

BillyBoy*. *Barbie: Her Life and Times.* Three Rivers Press. 1992.

Blitman, Joe. *Barbie and Her Mod, Mod, Mod, Mod World of Fashion.* Hobby House Press, 1996.

Blitman, Joe. *Francie & Her Mod, Mod, Mod World of Fashion.* Hobby House Press, 1996.

Cain Miller, Claire. "Barbie's New Job, Computer Engineer." *New York Times.* February 15, 2010. https://archive.nytimes.com/query.nytimes.com/gst/fullpage-9D03E3DB113BF936A25751C0A9669D8B63.html.

Carberry, James. "Valley of the Dolls." *Wall Street Journal.* June 20, 1973.

Carvajal, Doreen. "With Museum Shows in Europe, Barbie Gets Her Moment with the Masters." *New York Times.* March 11, 2016. https://www.nytimes.com/2016/03/11/arts/design/with-museum-shows-in-europe-barbie-gets-her-moment-with-the-masters.html

Clement, Douglas P. "The Female Identity, Discussed in Art." *New York Times.* April 3, 2016, https://www.nytimes.com/2016/04/03/nyregion/the-female-identity-discussed-in-art.html

Clifford, Stephanie. "More Dads Buy the Toys, So Barbie, and Stores, Get Makeovers." *New York Times.* December 4, 2012. https://www.nytimes.com/2012/12/04/business/more-dads-buy-the-toys-so-barbie-and-stores-get-makeovers.html

Creswell, Julie. "Mattel's Revival Plan: Bet on Barbie, the Movie." *New York Times.* December 13, 2018. https://www.nytimes.com/2018/12/13/business/mattel-barbie-movie-ynon-kreiz.html

D'Amato, Jennie. *Barbie: All Dolled Up: Celebrating 50 Years of Barbie.* Running Press, 2009.

Deutsch, Stefanie. Barbie: *The First 30 Years 1959 Through 1989: An Identification and Value Guide.* Collector Books, 1995.

Dockterman, Eliana. "Barbie's Got a New Body." *Time Magazine.* January 28, 2016.

Eagan, Cindy. *The Story of Barbie and the Woman Who Created Her.* Random House, 2017.

Elliott, Stuart. "Barbie's Sports Illustrated Swimsuit Issue Causes a Stir Online." *New York Times.* February 2, 2014. https://www.nytimes.com/2014/02/12/business/media/barbies-sports-illustrated-swimsuit-issue-causes-a-stir-online.html

Elliott, Stuart. "Leaving Behind Malibu in Search of a New Dream Home." *New York Times.* February 7, 2013, https://www.nytimes.com/2013/02/07/business/media/barbie-to-sell-her-malibu-dreamhouse.html

Fennick, Janine. *The Collectible Barbie Doll: An Illustrated Guide to Her Dreamy World.* Courage Books, 1996.

Fennick, Janine. *Identifying Barbie Dolls: The New Compact Study Guide and Identifier.* Hachette, 1998.

Friedman, Vanessa. "Ken's New Look(s), Deconstructed." *New York Times.* June 21, 2017. https://www.nytimes.com/2017/06/21/fashion/mattel-barbie-ken-dolls.html

Fury, Alexander. "In Paris, the Shoe Designer Who Collects Dolls." *New York Times.* October 5, 2016. https://www.nytimes.com/2016/10/05/t-magazine/fashion/fabrizio-viti-dolls-louis-vuitton-shoes-fashion-week.html

Gerber, Robin. *Barbie and Ruth: The Story of the World's Most Famous Doll and the Woman Who Created Her.* HarperCollins, 2008.

Glassenber, Abby. "Barbie Beginnings." *Sew News.* February-March, 2018.

Handler, Ruth. *Dream Doll: The Ruth Handler Story.* Longmeadow Press, 1995.

Hauser, Christine. "New Barbie Is Modeled After American Olympian Who Wears a Hijab." *New York Times.* November 14, 2017. https://www.nytimes.com/2017/11/14/business/barbie-hijab-ibtihaj-muhammad.html

Hazelhurst, Beatrice. "Tally of the Dolls." *New York Times.* October 30, 2018. https://www.nytimes.com/2018/10/30/style/instagram-dolls.html

Holder, Sandi. *Barbie: A Rare Beauty.* Krause Publications, 2010.

Itzkoff, Dave. "Barbie Heading to the Silver Screen." *New York Times.* September 25, 2009. https://archive.nytimes.com/query.nytimes.com/gst/fullpage-9C03E7D8153BF936A1575AC0A96F9C8B63.html.

James Shilkitus, Hillary. *The Complete & Unauthorized Guide to Vintage Barbie® Dolls: With Barbie®, Ken®, Francie®, Skipper® Fashions and the Whole Family.* Third edition. Schiffer, 2016.

James Shilkitus, Hillary. *It's All About the Accessories for the World's Most Fashionable Dolls, 1959–1972.* Third edition. Schiffer, 2016.

Kennedy, Randy. "Barbie, the Klimt Edition." *New York Times.* June 29, 2011. https://artsbeat.blogs.nytimes.com/2011/06/29/barbie-as-a-gustav-klimt-model.

Korbeck, Sharon. *The Best of Barbie: Four Decades of America's Favorite Doll.* Krause Publications, 2001.

Krier, Beth Ann. "Sweet 16: You've Come a Long Way, Barbie." *Los Angeles Times.* September 8, 1974.

Lambert, Molly. "Trixie Mattel Says Drag Queens Are Like Swiss Army Knives." *New York Times.* August 29, 2018. https://www.nytimes.com/2018/08/29/magazine/trixie-mattel-says-drag-queens-are-like-swiss-army-knives.html

Lord, M.G. *Forever Barbie: The Unauthorized Biography of a Real Doll.* Walker Books, 2004.

Lyons, Margaret. "How Much Watching Time Do You Have This Weekend?" *New York Times.* April 26, 2018. https://www.nytimes.com/2018/04/26/watching/what-to-watch-this-weekend-tv.html

Mallenbaum, Carly. "Barbie in 2018 and beyond: How the doll is getting more inclusive." *USA Today.* April 25, 2018

Martin, Judith. "Interview with a Superstar." *The Washington Post.* April 7, 1974

Masters, Kim. "Pretty, Plastic Barbie: Forever What We Make her." National Public Radio (NPR). March 9, 2008. https://www.npr.org/templates/story/story.php?storyId=87997519.

Melillo, Marcie. *The Ultimate Barbie Doll Book.* Krause Publications, 1996.

Montagne, Renee. "Bon Jour, Barbie! An American Icon Packs her Heels and Heads to France." National Public Radio (NPR). August 25, 2016. https://www.npr.org/templates/transcript/transcript.php?storyId=490948248.

Moore, Hannah. "Why Warhol painted Barbie." British Broadcasting Corporation (BBC). October 1, 2015. https://www.bbc.com/news/magazine-34407991.

Moynihan, Colin. "Frida Kahlo Is a Barbie Doll Now. (Signature Unibrow Not Included.)" *New York Times.* March 9, 2018. https://www.nytimes.com/2018/03/09/arts/design/frida-kahlo-barbie-mattel.html

Olds, Patrick C. *The Barbie Doll Years: A Comprehensive Listing & Value Guide of Dolls & Accessories.* Collector Books, 2006.

Olson, Elizabeth. "The Ken Doll Turns 50, and Wins a New Face." *New York Times.* March 22, 2011. https://www.nytimes.com/2011/03/22/business/media/22adco.html

Padnani, Amisha. "Sometimes It Is All Just Fun and Games." *New York Times.* May 11, 2017. https://www.nytimes.com/2017/05/11/business/stan-weston-gi-joe-barbie-frisbee-monopoly.html

Rana, Margo. *Collectibly Yours Barbie Doll 1980-1990: Identification & Price Guide.* Hobby House Press Inc., 1998.

Rogers, Mary F. *Barbie Culture.* SAGE Publications, 2000.

Ruby Lane. "How to Identify a Number One Barbie at the UFDC Doll Museum in Kansas City, Missouri." YouTube. April 2, 2017. https://www.youtube.com/watch?v=RkrK4lNo2pI.

Ruby Lane. "The History of the First Designer of the Barbie Doll: Charlotte Johnson." YouTube. April 14, 2017. https://www.youtube.com/watch?v=WmfWe6jVX9I.

Sarasohn-Kahn, Jane. *Contemporary Barbie Dolls: 1980 And Beyond.* Antique Trader Books, 1997.

Schmid, Cornelius. "6 Holiday Toy Crazes and Why They Captivated Kids (and Parents)." *New York Times.* December 21, 2017. https://www.nytimes.com/2017/12/21/us/christmas-toys.html?

Selin Davis, Lisa. "Like Tomboys and Hate Girlie Girls? That's Sexist." *New York Times.* December 19, 2018. https://www.nytimes.com/2018/12/19/opinion/tomboys-girlie-girls-sexism.html

Shilkitus James, Hillary. *The Complete and Unauthorized Guide to Vintage Barbie Dolls: With Barbie & Skipper Fashions and the Whole Family of Barbie Dolls.* Second Edition. Schiffer Publishing, 2011.

Singer, Natasha. "A Wi-Fi Barbie Doll with the Soul of Siri." *New York Times.* March 29, 2015. https://www.nytimes.com/2015/03/29/technology/a-wi-fi-barbie-doll-with-the-soul-of-siri.html

Singleton, Bridget. *The Art of Barbie.* Vision on, March 2000.

Sink Eames, Sarah. *Barbie Fashion: The Complete History of the Wardrobes of Barbie Doll, Her Friends, and Her Family, Vol. 1: 1959–1967.* Collector Books, 1990.

Spigel, Lynn. *Welcome to the Dreamhouse: Popular Media and Postwar Suburbs.* Duke University Press, 2001

St. John Dewein, Sibyl. *The Collector's Encyclopedia of Barbie Dolls and Collectibles.* Collector Books, 1984.

Stone, Tanya Lee. *The Good, the Bad, and the Barbie: A Doll's History and Her Impact on Us.* Viking, 2010.

Supreme, Jpegger. "Stanley Colorite AKA Barbie Man's World Largest Barbie Collection." Jpegy. 2014. http://jpegy.com/geeky/stanley-colorite-aka-barbie-mans-world-largest-barbie-collection-18165.

Tosa, Marco. *Barbie: Four Decades of Fashion, Fantasy, and Fun.* Harry N. Abrams Inc., 1998.

Verbeten, Sharon. *Warman's Barbie Doll Field Guide: Values and Identification.* Krause Publications, 2009.

Vlahos, James. "Barbie Wants to Get to Know Your Child." *New York Times.* September 20, 2015. https://www.nytimes.com/2015/09/20/magazine/barbie-wants-to-get-to-know-your-child.html

Vora, Shivani. "Tour and Hotel News: Barbie in Montreal; Cooking in Chile." *New York Times.* March 9, 2016. https://www.nytimes.com/2016/03/09/travel/tour-and-hotel-news-barbie-in-montreal-cooking-in-chile.html

Westenhouser, Kitturah B. *The Story of Barbie.* Collector Books, 1994.

Wichter, Zach. "10 Hot Toys That Changed the Way People Play." *New York Times.* December 9, 2017. https://www.nytimes.com/2017/12/09/business/10-hot-toys-play.html

Zeldis McDonough, Yona. *The Barbie Chronicles: A Living Doll Turns Forty.* Touchstone, 1999.

ABOVE: Original Mattel sketch for Barbie's attire known as Red Sheath Sensation Dress, which was produced from 1961 to 1964.

ACKNOWLEDGMENTS

Many thanks to my smart, patient, and enthusiastic editor Bonnie Honeycutt. She guided this book with skill and good humor.

The stellar staff at the Barbie brand were a joy to interview, and showed enormous generosity in answering questions, explaining the intricacies and evolution of the brand, and in sharing their personal stories. Particular thanks to: Lisa McKnight, Kim Culmone, Michelle Chidoni, Robert Best, Matt Repicky, and Liz Maglione. This book was also greatly enriched by help from Bill Greening, Brand Historian, and Eliana Ruiz, Archivist, who continue to do important work in archiving the documentary and visual history of Barbie. Their help was invaluable.

Special thanks to Kitturah Westenhouser, who shared her tape recordings of Ruth Handler from the early 1990s, and whose *The Story of Barbie* (1994 and 1999 editions) remains a treasure trove of information and historical photographs. Thanks also to Bradley Justice, who has done amazing work in unearthing the story of Charlotte Johnson, and who helped with many questions I had along the way. Every interviewee shared their love of all things Barbie with passion and clarity. Thank you all!

Finally, my husband, Tony Records, gave the kind of support, good humor, and love that I've been privileged to enjoy for thirty years. If I'm lucky, we'll get another thirty years, like Ruth and Elliot Handler!

ABOUT THE AUTHOR

Robin Gerber is a best-selling author and historian. She is the author of *Leadership the Eleanor Roosevelt Way: Timeless Strategies from the First Lady of Courage*. Her most recent book is the first biography of the founder of Mattel, Ruth Handler, titled *Barbie and Ruth: The Story of the World's Most Famous Doll and the Woman Who Created Her*. Her articles have appeared in *USA Today*, the *Washington Post*, *The Philadelphia Inquirer*, and numerous other newspapers and magazines. Prior to becoming an author, Robin practiced law in Washington, D.C., and worked on Capitol Hill. She has studied and written about leadership development since 1975.

OPPOSITE: A portrait of Ruth and Elliott Handler holding a Barbie and Ken doll, on February 12, 1987. The couple received their second Lifetime Achievement Award from *Doll Reader* magazine.

ABOVE: Mattel's President 2000 Barbie was sold exclusively at Toys "R" Us stores with a nationwide movement aimed at inspiring and educating young people about their right to vote, and also emphasizing the importance of women in politics. President 2000 Barbie comes dressed in a blue skirt with matching jacket, and also comes with an additional red gown, shown here.

IMAGE CREDITS

Cover: © Mattel
Endpapers: © Mattel
Page 2: © Mattel
Page 5: © Mattel
Page 6: © Mattel
Page 8: © Mattel
Page 10: © Mattel
Page 12-13: © Mattel
Page 14 : © Mattel
Page 15: © Mattel
Page 16: © Mattel
Page 17: © Mattel
Page 18: © Mattel
Page 19: © Mattel
Page 20: © Found Image Holdings/Corbis via Getty Images
Page 21: © Mattel
Page 22: © Mattel
Page 23: © Mattel
Page 24: © Mattel
Page 25: © Mattel
Page 26: © Sueddeutsche Zeitung Photo/Alamy
Page 27: © SSPL/Getty Images
Page 28: © Mattel
Page 29: © Mattel
Page 30: © Mattel
Page 31: © Mattel
Page 32: © Mattel
Page 33: © Mattel
Page 34: © Mattel
Page 35: © Mattel
Page 36: © Courtesy of Bradley Justice
Page 37: © Mattel
Page 38-39: © Tony Korody/Getty Images
Page 40: © Don Bartletti/Getty Images
Page 42: (Top) © CBS Photo Archive/Getty Images; (Bottom) © Larry Ellis/Stringer via Getty Images
Page 43 :© Mattel
Page 44: © Mattel
Page 45: © Mattel
Page 46: © Mattel
Page 47: © Mattel
Page 48: © Mattel
Page 49: © Mattel
Page 50: © Courtesy of Bradley Justice
Page 51: (Top) © Mattel; © Courtesy of Bradley Justice
Page 52: © Courtesy of Bradley Justice
Page 53: © Courtesy of Bradley Justice
Page 54: © Mattel
Page 55: (Top) © Keystone-France/Getty Images; (Bottom) © Mattel
Page 56: © Mattel
Page 57: © Mattel
Page 58: © Courtesy of Bradley Justice
Page 59: © Courtesy of Bradley Justice
Page 60: © Courtesy of Bradley Justice

Page 61: © Courtesy of Bradley Justice
Page 62-63: © ullstein bild Dtl./Getty Images
Page 64: © Keystone-France/Getty Images
Page 66: © Mattel
Page 67: © Mattel
Page 68: © Mattel
Page 69: © Mattel
Page 70-71: © Mattel
Page 72: © Mattel
Page 73: © Mattel
Page 74: © Mattel
Page 75: © David M. Benett/Getty Images
Page 76: © Mattel
Page 77: © Mattel
Page 78: © Mattel
Page 79: © Mattel
Page 80-81: © Mattel
Page 82: © Mattel
Page 84: © Mattel
Page 85: © Mattel
Page 86: © Mattel
Page 87: © Mattel
Page 88: © Mattel
Page 89: © Mattel
Page 89: (Left and middle) © Mattel; (Right) ©
Page 90: © Mattel
Page 91: © Mattel
Page 92: © Mattel
Page 93: © Mattel
Page 94: © Mattel
Page 95: © Mattel
Page 96: © Mattel
Page 97: © Mattel
Page 98-99: © Mattel
Page 100: © Mattel
Page 102: © Mattel
Page 103: © Mattel
Page 104: © Mattel
Page 105: © Peter Bischoff/Stringer via Getty Images
Page 106: © Mattel
Page 107: © Mattel
Page 108-109: © Mattel
Page 110: © Pierre Vauthey/Getty Images
Page 112: © Luci Nicholson/Stringer via Getty Images
Page 113: © Mattel
Page 114: (Top) © Daniel Simon/Getty Images; (Bottom) © Bruce Glikas/Getty Images
Page 115: © Michael Tran/Getty Images
Page 116: © Johnny Green-PA Images via Getty Images
Page 117: (Left) ©PA Images/Alamy; (Right) © Mattel
Page 118: © Cassy Cohen/Getty Images
Page 119: © Gilles Bassignac/Getty Images
Page 120: © Gilles Bassignac/Getty Images
Page 121: © Venturelli/Getty Images
Page 122: (Top) © Lawrence Lucier/Stringer via Getty Images; (Bottom) © Timur Emek/Getty Images
Page 123: (Top) © Time & Life Pictures/Getty Images;

(Bottom) © Venturelli/Getty Images
Page 124: © Mattel
Page 125: © Mattel
Page 126: © Stephen Chernin/Getty Images
Page 127: © DMI/Getty Images
Page 128: © Timothy A. Clary/Getty Images
Page 129: © Timothy A. Clary/Getty Images
Page 130: (Left) © Scott Gries/Getty Images; (Right) © Getty Images
Page 131: (Top) © Mirrorpix/Getty Images; (Bottom) © Pascal Le Segretain/Getty Images
Page 132: © Mattel
Page 133: © Mattel
Page 134: Photos by Robert Ryan/Courtesy of Corazon Ugalde Yellen Armenta
Page 135: © Matthew Fearn-PA Images via Getty Images
Page 136: © Robin Marchant/Getty Images
Page 137: © Michael Crabtree-PA Images via Getty Images
Page 138: © The AGE/Getty Images
Page 139: © The AGE/Getty Images
Page 140: (Left) © Donato Sardella/Getty Images; (Right) © Ron Galella/Getty Images
Page 141: (Left) © Dave Allocca/Getty Images; (Right) © Deborah Feingold/Getty Images
Page 142-143: © Mattel
Page 144: © Lawrence Lucier/Stringer via Getty Images
Page 146: © Chesnot/Getty Images
Page 147: Courtesy of Jian Yang
Page 148: Courtesy of Jian Yang
Page 149: Courtesy of Jian Yang
Page 150: © Kevin Winter/Getty Images
Page 151: © Paolo Bona/Shutterstock
Page 152: © chrisdorney/Shutterstock
Page 153: © Courtesy of Grace Mulgrew from Grace's World
Page 154: © Mattel
Page 155: © Mattel
Page 156: © Barcroft Media/Getty Images
Page 157: © Barcroft Media/Getty Images
Page 158: © Presley Ann/Stringer via Getty Images
Page 159: © Barcroft Media/Getty Images
Page 160-161: © Alexander Tamargo/Getty Images
Page 162: © Robert Mora/ Getty Images
Page 164: © Hector Mata/Getty Images
Page 165: (Top) © Courtesy of Kitturah Westenhouser; (Bottom) © Don Bartletti/Getty Images
Page 166: © picture alliance/Getty Images
Page 168-169: © Chesnot/Getty Images
Page 171: © Mattel
Page 172: © Bettmann/Getty Images
Page 173: Courtesy of Robin Gerber
Page 174 © Yvonne Hemsey/Getty Images
Timeline images: © Mattel

A BRIEF HISTORY OF

Barbie ™

INSPIRING GIRLS SINCE 1959

Founded by Ruth Handler—businesswoman, mom, and pioneer of her time—Barbie has been breaking boundaries and sparking imaginations since her debut. See Barbie's journey throughout the past six decades.

SIGN LANGUAGE BARBIE

In 2001, Sign Language Teacher Barbie empowered girls to learn new languages. Her hand was molded into the ASL sign for "I love you," and she came with illustrations of common words in sign language and fingerspelling for each letter of the alphabet.

PALEONTOLOGIST BARBIE

In 1997, Paleontologist Barbie inspired girls to discover new things—like hidden fossils! With her cool dinosaur-themed outfit and accessories, Paleontologist Barbie was ready to dig up some fun.

FIRST FEATURE-LENGTH FILM

In 2001, Barbie starred in her first feature-length film, Barbie™ in *The Nutcracker*, on CBS. The movie tells the tale of Clara and her amazing nutcracker, who set off on an adventure to find the Sugarplum Princess. Barbie shows girls that if you are kind, clever, and brave, anything is possible.

WINTER SPORTS BARBIE

In 1995, Barbie encouraged girls to explore a range of winter sports including snowboarding, which was predominately an all-male sport at the time. With Winter Sports Barbie, girls could imagine hitting the slopes and carving up some fresh powder.

1995   1997   2000   2001   2002

AVIATOR BARBIE

In 2002, Aviator Barbie took girls' imaginations to new heights. Dressed in a cool flight suit and helmet, she was ready for any mission or rescue effort. She inspired future aviators to play out their dreams of soaring through the sky.

EXTREME 360° BARBIE

In 2000, Extreme 360° Barbie inspired girls to go big. She came with a skateboard, rollerblades, and had bendable limbs so she could do awesome tricks.

FIREFIGHTER BARBIE

In 1995, Firefighter Barbie showed girls they could be everyday heroes. With her yellow firefighter uniform and helmet, girls could imagine putting out fires and saving the day.

BUILDER BARBIE

In 2017, Builder Barbie introduced girls to the world of construction and inspired them to build big dreams. With her hardhat, toolbelt, and building blocks, Barbie was ready to create worlds where anything is possible.

BARBIE DREAMHOUSE ADVENTURES

In 2018, the animated series *Barbie Dreamhouse Adventures* was released on Netflix. The hilarious and heartwarming series let fans peek into the everyday life of Barbie as she embarked on exciting adventures with her family, friends, and Ken!

#MOREROLEMODELS

Barbie shined a light on empowering role models from the past and present in an effort to inspire more girls. The campaign, #MoreRoleModels, honored extraordinary women from around the world on International Women's Day. The Inspiring Women doll line also launched and featured Frida Kahlo, Katherine Johnson, and Amelia Earhart.

60TH ANNIVERSARY

Since 1959, Barbie has been inspiring girls to be anything. From princess to president, astronaut to zoologist, there isn't a plastic ceiling Barbie hasn't broken. Today, with over 200 careers and counting, she continues to inspire the limitless potential in every girl.

2017   2018   2019

BEEKEEPER BARBIE

In 2018, Beekeeper Barbie was released to teach the next generation about the importance of bees and how to care for them. Equipped with her beekeeping suit, Barbie was ready to raise her hive and harvest honey.

DREAM GAP PROJECT

Barbie launched the Dream Gap Project, an ongoing global initiative that gives girls the resources and support they need to continue to believe they can be anything. The initiative includes funding research, highlighting positive role models, and producing content and products that inspire girls.

THE NEW CREW

In 2017, the Barbie Fashionistas crew became more diverse than ever before, featuring more skin tones, eye colors, hairstyles, and fashions. Ken also got an update, with two more body types added to the lineup: broad and slim. #NextGenKen had a variety of new looks including a man bun, cornrows, and freckles.

BARBIE + TYNKER

In 2018, Barbie encouraged girls to explore STEM through imaginative play and a partnership with Tynker, the award-winning computing platform. With the Robotics Engineer Barbie doll and You Can Be Anything programming lessons, girls learned about coding while discovering new careers.